THE BAREFOOT SURGEON

The inspirational story of Dr Sanduk Ruit,
the eye surgeon giving sight and hope
to the world's poor

ALI GRIPPER

ALLEN&UNWIN
SYDNEY·MELBOURNE·AUCKLAND·LONDON

First published in 2018

Copyright © Ali Gripper 2018

Allen & Unwin
83 Alexander Street
Crows Nest NSW 2065
Australia
Phone: (61 2) 8425 0100
Email: info@allenandunwin.com
Web: www.allenandunwin.com

A catalogue record for this book is available from the National Library of Australia

ISBN 978 1 76029 270 6

Set in 12/18 pt Sabon by Midland Typesetters, Australia
Printed and bound in Australia by Griffin Press
10 9 8 7 6 5 4 3 2

The paper in this book is FSC® certified. FSC® promotes environmentally responsible, socially beneficial and economically viable management of the world's forests.

CONTENTS

For Tuomo

'Ruit doesn't overdo it with words and conversation. He's quite sober in the way he interacts with people, but what people pick up is the quality of his presence, someone who is enormously competent. When you are with him, and working with him, there's a feeling of trust and confidence that comes from his very being. It's something that's hard to describe, but which everyone feels somehow when they are with him. The fact that he travels so far with the patients to be with them characterises a truly compassionate person. It's not about being sentimental, or sitting around thinking *I'd really like to make a difference*. He just gets up and does it, to places such as North Korea, because he knows how terrible it must be for the blind there. He never thinks at all about how he can make a good impression. What he always asks himself is how he can make a difference, with the means he has, and the skills he has, and the capacity he has. He succeeds because he has no agenda other than to help people. It's a great joy to be with him, there's a sense of deep complicity, of working for the same purpose, without having to talk about it.'

— Matthieu Ricard, Buddhist monk and French writer

'As Henry Ford changed the world by making an automobile affordable for ordinary Americans, Ruit changed the world by devising an ingenious surgical technique and procedure that made sight restoring intraocular lens implant cataract surgery possible for people everywhere. Even for the poorest people living in remote villages.'

— Garry Brian, Australian ophthalmologist

'Fred Hollows and Sanduk Ruit were true soul mates. But now here is Ruit, a couple of decades later, and he's gone out and he's actually done it. It was Fred's imprimatur that got him launched, but Ruit just kept plugging away. He raised the money, built the hospital, trained the surgeons, and held the camps. Ruit has almost halved blindness in Nepal and is spreading his technique to other countries. It's amazing to think that, in my lifetime, or in my children's lifetime, we will see cataract blindness ended. People will keep getting cataracts—it's part of the ageing process—but Ruit and the army of surgeons he's training are putting a lid on it. What Ruit has achieved is well beyond Fred's wildest dreams. Ruit went on to become a God-like figure who looks after the blind. He reminds me a lot of one of the other remarkable men I've interviewed, Don Bradman. They both have a God-given talent and skill that they both have harnessed in a highly disci-plined way. Bradman had no ego at all; he just knew he was a fantastic batsman. Ruit is also clearly a man without ego and a man with immense self-respect. He doesn't need to boast about how good he was. He didn't ever need to tell people he was a brilliant surgeon, he just is. He's very humble but he certainly knows his place in medicine. He doesn't dismiss winning the Nobel Prize as ridiculous. He's got great self-respect. I've covered so many fascinating stories in my life and I'll never forget the joy on the patients' faces at an eye camp

Ruit held in Myanmar a few years ago. Ruit did 600 oper-ations that week and there was this incredible collective joy as he looked at the rows and rows of his patients who could see again and who were absolutely jubilant. They just sort of broke into dance and song. The surgeons watching him work were just in wonderment at the pace and meticulousness of his surgery. He is just so fast. We put a clock on him to watch him—he was doing operations in about five minutes, and the other doctors were doing it in about 15 minutes. It was just astonishing to stand there and watch.'

— Ray Martin, Australian journalist

PROLOGUE

The morning sun was just beginning to light up the snow peaks of the Himalayas in north-eastern Nepal as Kanchi Maya's brother brought her to the small community eye centre. In the custom of the region, he carried his adult sister on his back in a large wicker basket, attached to his forehead on a tumpline—a mode of transport known as 'basket taxi'. Kanchi was in patched clothes, her body rail-thin from malnutrition. After her brother lowered her onto the ground, she shuffled timidly with bare feet toward the eye camp, holding her brother's hand for support. Beside her was her young daughter, who carried her sickly baby brother. Despite being swaddled tightly in a blanket, the one-year-old boy looked close to perishing.

One of the assistants gently led Kanchi to Dr Sanduk Ruit's operating table. He asked her how she made a living. Shaking with nerves, she whispered that she had been trying to support her children by growing maize and tending goats. She'd been blind in both eyes for almost four years and had never seen her son. Like so many blind women in the developing world, she had been rejected by her husband and his family after she had lost her sight and was no longer useful. She'd been taken in by her brother instead.

Ruit examined her eyes, which were clouded with the large pearly discs that signify advanced cataracts. He knew that if the operation went well, Kanchi would be able to see clearly the next day. An anaesthetic block was given under the sides of her eyes. Half an hour later, a nurse swabbed the rust-brown antiseptic over Kanchi's eyes and draped a green cloth with a hole cut out around the eyes. 'Don't be scared,' Ruit told her, as he separated her eyelids open with a small wire speculum, and then patted her gently on the shoulder. 'There is no pain, and I'm going to give you your sight back.'

He lowered the microscope over her eye and went to work. He quickly removed the first cataract, as hard as a walnut, and replaced it with a plastic intraocular lens, which had been specially measured for her, smaller than a contact lens. The incision he made in her eye was so small and delicate that it would seal without stitches the next day.

Ten minutes later, the assistant lifted Kanchi up, turned her around and then lay her down on the other side of the table so Ruit could operate on her second eye. Once it was over, Kanchi shuffled out, led by two assistants, to the recovery room, where she and her family were served the local staple dinner of *dal bhat*—lentil soup and rice—washed down with cups of *chia* the sweet, milky spiced tea the Nepalese drink all day.

Kanchi's reaction the next morning, as the bandages and plastic caps over her eyes were removed, was spellbinding.

At first, she squinted, looking confused as she tried to take in her surroundings. As her line of sight extended and the realisation dawned that she could see, tears of joy rolled down her broad cheeks. Ruit lifted Kanchi's baby out of his cradle and into her arms. She held her little boy up close to her face, looked at him incredulously, and kissed him softly. She was too overcome to talk, but her face, alight with love and wonder, told a thousand words. 'Seeing Kanchi kissing her baby, that's what sight is all about, it's all about seeing loved ones again properly,' Ruit says.

The surgeon's smile that day was as broad as Kanchi's. After more than 120,000 similar operations in Nepal, and hundreds of similar outreach camps throughout the world; after being showered with awards and accolades for pioneering this unique, small-incision cataract surgery, it is still his patients' beaming faces that gives Ruit the greatest satisfaction in life. What he loves, more than anything else in the world, is giving the gift of sight to people who would otherwise have been completely overlooked, and who are sometimes left in back rooms to die.

He knows only too well that being blind in a country like Nepal absolutely devastates the lives of people like Kanchi. The steep, narrow mountain roads are dangerous to navigate. The blind have no braille, no guide dogs, no white canes, and no special schools. They often cannot afford the bus fare to Kathmandu or a local clinic. Despite the image of village life as a supportive community, the harsh reality in countries like Nepal is that, if the blind cannot contribute to their family's subsistence farm, they are often shunned as just another mouth to feed.

For more than three decades, Ruit's mission has been to take his life-transforming operations to the blind. He calls them 'children of a lesser God'. No road has ever been too far or too steep.

Kanchi could easily have been Ruit's sister, his mother, his aunt or his neighbour. Ruit knows these people; he has lived their life.

1

OUT OF THIN AIR

Sanduk was born in 1954, several hundred kilometres away from the eye camp Kanchi was brought to, in the ice-encrusted village of Olanchungola, 3200 metres above sea level in north-eastern Nepal.

The village of 200 people lay huddled in the Tamor Gorge, in the lee of Kanchenjunga, the third highest mountain in the world. Walung, as the village was also known, had been home to the Walunga tribe, who had settled there after migrating from Tibet seven generations previously. It's one of the most desolate and isolated places in the world. Taplejung, the nearest large town, is four days' walk away, due south. On top of a hill swathed in giant rhododendrons, Sanduk's family would visit the 500-year-old monastery, Diki Choeling, one of the oldest in the nation. The only thing beyond the monastery were the Himalayas.

Sanduk was born in the lowest tier of a rigid class system, with absolutely nothing to his name, no money and no connections. His father, Sonam Wangul Ruit (the family added 'Ruit' to their surname 'Wangul', when they moved to Kathmandu in the 1960s, after their ancestors from the village of Ruthok in Tibet), is one of the few people left in the world who can tell you stories about yetis, the half-man, half-beast said to inhabit the high snowfields of north-eastern Nepal. With only half his teeth, almost completely deaf and a blanket wrapped around his knees, 90-year-old Sonam can give an impersonation of the large, upright creature's high-pitched cry that will make every hair on the back of your neck stand on end. Although almost half a century ago, Sonam's close encounters with the abominable snowmen are still fresh in his mind. 'They were very big but very shy. They scuttled behind rocks whenever we came close.'

As a travel-hardened salt trader who spent his working life making the dangerous trip up to Tibet through the Himalayas, Sonam had plenty of stories for his son when he returned home. Sanduk would listen wide-eyed with wonder as his father told him about skirmishes with bandits, using guns and knives that he kept hidden in saddle bags. He told his son about the giant cairns of prayer stones, carved with the ancient Buddhist blessing *Om Mani Padme Hum*, which means 'may the guru remain in your heart forevermore'.

His father gave accounts of the elusive snow leopards, black bears, blue sheep and flying squirrels renowned in the region. He told him about the 'little folk', men less than one-foot high living in remote gorges. And about the yogis living in caves set high up in the cliffs, who had practised meditation for so long that they had mastered the art of levitation.

Sonam shared these anecdotes about his caravan trade around the hearth of his family's simple timber house in

Walung, topped with prayer flags. They were stories of a unique, almost mythical world which has since disappeared.

Despite the sub-zero temperatures and knee-high snow throughout the winter, the village had survived for centuries because it was the stepping stone to a trade route between Nepal and Tibet. Sonam and the other traders would be away for months at a time, bringing back hand-woven carpets, wool, turquoise, coral and, most importantly, hessian bags crammed with salt. On their return, after staying home in Walung for two or three nights, they would head south, selling these precious goods in Nepal and further afield in Calcutta, India. Months later, they would return with coveted possessions from the subcontinent: grain, paint, biscuits, dyes and cooking equipment.

Sonam's livelihood came to an end after China began occupying Tibet in the 1950s, when the smaller passes were closed and trade was diverted to larger, more official routes near Kathmandu. But before that, these slow, swaying processions of yaks and dzos (a Tibetan-bred half-cow, half-yak), were the villagers' only connection with the outside world. Like all the other children in the village, Sanduk regarded the traders as swashbuckling heroes; they would arrive wearing thick mountaineering goggles on their shaggy ponies, bringing clouds of dust and fabulous tales from afar. Their arrival was the main event in town. Everyone would cram onto their timber verandas as soon they heard the jangling chorus of yak bells, whistles and shouts that would herald their arrival.

Sonam was the last of six generations who had plied their trade between Tibet and Calcutta after migrating to Walung. Like his forebears, he survived through rugged practicality, physical strength, and a reputation for straightforwardness in his dealings with everybody.

In 1950, when he was 25, Sonam married a striking, quietly confident 20-year-old woman named Kasang Doma Ukyab. Kasang was the daughter of the head of the village, Goba Dorji Namgyal Ukyab, otherwise known as 'Goba'. The Ukyab family had also lived in Walung for more than six generations after migrating from Tibet.

But, like so many other families living in a remote community far from medical care, tragedy struck relentlessly. When Sonam and Kasang's first son was three years old, an epidemic of diarrhoea swept through the community. Sanduk's elder brother was one of its victims. Being devout Buddhists, his heartbroken parents went to the village monastery every day to pray for another son. When Kasang gave birth to another boy a year later, in 1954, they felt he was the answer to their prayers. As she was in labour, Kasang remembers having a vision of a bright blue sky filled with fluttering white ceremonial scarves. Seeing this as an auspicious sign, she named him Sanduk, or 'Dragon of the Sky'. He was to be powerful, this one.

As was the custom of that era, Sonam, being the second son in his family, was originally destined to become a Buddhist monk. He did spend several years steeped in monastic life, but the death of his elder brother meant he ended up joining his father as a salt trader instead. Those years immersed in the teachings and practice of Buddhism made a lasting impression on him; for the rest of his life, his devotion to the teachings has remained unshaken. One of Sanduk's first memories is waking before dawn to the sound of his father's soft chanting and the comforting clicking of his *mala*, or wooden prayer beads. Every morning and evening, Sonam would sit at his small shrine next to the fireplace, praying to the Dalai Lama and his main teacher, Guru Rinpoche, one of the most powerful figures in the Buddhist faith, revered for bringing Buddhism to Tibet in the 9th century.

Despite the fact that Sonam took his responsibilities as a father seriously, his relationship with his son was never particularly affectionate. He was much more of a strict, controlling autocrat, someone Sanduk both feared and revered.

'When I was mischievous and misbehaved—which was often—Sonam would whip the back of my legs with wet nettle leaves,' he says. 'It stung like crazy.'

'I was naughty, no doubt about that. When I broke my right arm, skylarking about on the back of a dzo, the monks wrapped it up tightly in a bamboo splint. But I couldn't wait to throw stones at the peach and walnut trees again, so I started using my left arm instead.'

Within a week after his accident, Sanduk became ambidextrous, using his left hand for rough or heavy work, and his right for fine detail and precision—a tremendous occupational bonus for a future surgeon.

Photographs from that time show Sonam to be a man of noble bearing, sporting a moustache and a long woollen tunic and hat, his long black hair tied back with ribbons. On special occasions, he would don gold earrings.

Despite Sonam's gruffness, he taught his children to be gentle with all living creatures. 'He would save the life of a beetle, or an ant, if he had to,' Sanduk says. 'He'd pick tiny creatures up from stone paths to save them from being trodden on. He had an old mule which he patted and kept downstairs behind our home, even though it was of no use as a packhorse anymore.'

Even more intimidating than his father was Sanduk's maternal grandfather, Goba. He was a legendary figure, the unofficial magistrate of the village. 'He would deliver justice from the veranda of his house, handing out punishments off the top of his head. He'd yell out "Give him 50 whips!" to an accused man brought before him, often with his hands tied behind him. Or he'd say, "Make him pay this much as a fine!" We were all absolutely terrified of him.'

Shut off from the rest of the world, life carried on in Walung implacably, as it had for centuries. There was no television, no electricity, no telephone and no radio. And there was no access to a medical clinic, doctor, hospital, or even traditional healers.

'If someone contracted a serious disease, they spent their remaining time waiting to die,' he recalls. Sanduk's home was like all the others in the village; the ground floor was for storing stacks of firewood, giant hessian bags of salt, and dried animal dung that would be used for fuel. A slippery, steep log ladder led to the first floor, where an open fire was always burning or flickering; at night, the coals were left to smoulder, and the fire was lit first thing in the morning. Kasang would cook potatoes with cheese, porridge, or brew salted butter tea. To one side was a giant copper jar used to store water, and behind it was a cupboard for precious belongings such as new clothes, biscuits, chocolate, and candles made out of vegetable oil.

On the upstairs veranda, a sprig of juniper would be

burning aromatically. Once a month Kasang would bathe Sanduk, gently pouring warm water from a saucepan over her son as he sat on the veranda.

Every sound Sanduk heard, save the *grong-grong* of the yak's bells and the constant chanting and drum beats from the monastery, was that of nature: the rushing of the Tamor River, the caw of black crows, the wind in the birch and juniper trees, the crackle of fire. Elsewhere in the world, giant technological strides were being made. Russia and the United States were launching their first astronauts into space. Wealthy Londoners and New Yorkers were crossing the Atlantic on the first passenger jet planes. Sanduk and his siblings and friends heard about these great events from the magazines the yak traders unpacked from their saddle bags after they had returned from India.

But what his family lacked in material goods and modern technology was made up for with a sense of being deeply loved. His mother was fiercely protective of Sanduk because of what had happened to her firstborn. 'She brought me up on biscuits and chocolates,' Sanduk is fond of saying.

In the winter, as the temperature plummeted below zero for months on end, icicles would encrust the village houses. The drinking water would freeze, and the mighty Tamor River that rushed through the village became grey with melted glacial water. The days were short. The family would rise at dawn, spend much of the day sitting on low benches around the fire, wrapped in quilts and blankets, and go to bed when night fell. At night, Sonam would sit on the end of his bed by the fire, with a yak blanket around his knees, sipping *tongba*, a homemade brew of warm fermented millet renowned for warding off the cold and altitude sickness. Kasang would spin wool and weave cloth.

'She was always dressed in a silk blouse under a traditional Tibetan tunic, and the striped apron or *pangi* that all the married women wore. She wore a yak's wool jumper in the winter, and her hair was centrally parted, with plaits on either side. She was very dignified and quiet. She was very devoted to us,' he says.

Sanduk used to share a mattress with her in one corner of the living room, and his father would sleep in the other corner. They slept under thick, padded quilts made out of yak wool known as *chuktuks*. 'It was very cosy because we'd all be sleeping around the fire, listening to the roar of the Tamor River outside.'

Although they didn't display their affection, and it was an arranged marriage, there was undoubtedly love between his parents. Whenever traders came through the town, Kasang would bail them up, anxious for news of her husband. 'Where did you meet him?' she'd ask. 'How was he? Where was he? Was he in good health?'

Sanduk's older cousin, Tenzing Ukyab, who grew up with him in Olanchungola (known locally as 'Gola'), recalls, 'She was a very loving person, especially to me, as well as her own children. She was very confident of herself, just like her father. She commanded respect from all. She was very good looking as a young lady and was always dignified and gracious as she grew older.' After Ukyab lost his mother, he regarded Kasang as his guardian and would ask her for advice. 'She didn't receive any formal education but she was extremely intelligent and thoughtful.'

Sanduk's maternal grandmother doted on him too. 'She called me *bhu*, which means 'little son', and she'd also spoil me with lollies. I remember lying in bed with her as she sang lullabies to me.'

His younger sister Yangla, born two years later in 1956, was his first childhood companion. They played long imaginative games on the rocks by the river, cuddled the toy-like baby dzos or disappeared into the rhododendron forest for hours. Later, Kasang gave birth to another daughter, Chhengjing, in 1959; a son, Ladenla, in 1962; and a third daughter, Chundak, in 1963. But it was Yangla, with her pretty dark plaits, curious nature and melodious singing, who always had a special place in Sanduk's heart.

The Diki Choeling monastery was where the villagers took their newborn babies to be blessed, where they married, and where they were cremated. Like most monasteries in northern Nepal, it was decorated with *thangkas* or cloth paintings depicting the hell realms and scowling wrathful gods. Sanduk found it eerie as a boy.

'When I went inside the monastery, I was always scared of the sound resonating on the walls of the monks chanting, and the smell of incense burning. The paintings on the wall had skeletons on them that seemed to stare right at you.'

But Ruit's view of the monastery improved when he burnt his hand badly as a toddler, impetuously plunging his forearm into a pot of boiling water one day, deep in the middle of winter. He remembers his mother panicking, and his father carrying him frantically in his arms to the monastery where the monks wrapped his raw arm in butter and a shawl and said a special prayer ceremony for him. Their compassion and care and their deep faith and conviction in the healing qualities of the prayers left an abiding impression on him.

During the spring festival of Losar (meaning 'new year') and Futuk, when the monks performed traditional dances with masks outside the monastery, Gola seemed like a heavenly place to the boy. 'We'd sit in the sunshine in new clothes, spreading out carpets from our home, enjoying picnics, watching the festivities. We looked forward to these special days all year.'

But despite the idyllic simplicity of the mountain village, there was one major drawback—there was no school. For a boy with an inquiring mind, this would prove to be a major problem. 'I always felt a bit different from other people because I was so inquisitive,' he recalls. 'I'd ask, "Why is the river flowing this way?"; "Why does the snow come at this time?"; "How do the eagles fly so high?"; "What makes a plane work?"'

But he didn't really receive any full answers. There was very little information from the outside world.

His cousin Ukyab had no idea back then that Sanduk would go on to become a giant of Asia. What he remembers vividly is the two of them running wild and free on his family's farm, picking berries, swimming in the streams, and playing pranks with a sling shot, as well as bows and arrows, shooting the arrows right up to the roof. 'He always had a strong arm with the slingshot in our village,' Ukyab says. 'Of course, now he uses it for his lightning-fast operations. We all thought he'd do something far more adventurous with his life, like become a pilot.'

It didn't take Sanduk's father long to see that his son was different to the other boys. Sonam's years in the monastery and his travels afield to Calcutta and Llasa in Tibet gave him a keen appreciation of the power of education. He organised for a customs official to teach Sanduk rudimentary Nepalese, English and maths. Even then, it became clear that Sanduk was too bright to spend his days as a salt trader.

It was rare for families to send their children away from the village, but Sonam knew instinctively the village was too small and stifling a place for his son to grow up. He needed to be enrolled in a proper school. 'He has to go south, to Darjeeling,' Sanduk overheard Goba say to his parents. 'This boy is not going to do anything good here other than cause mischief.'

Too shy to ask, Sanduk desperately wanted to know where he was being sent, and for how long. 'I had a vague under-standing that it was going to be a long trip. Part of me was curious about "going south", as they called it, and another part was afraid of leaving home.'

As the day drew closer, Kasang started slowly putting special things in a bag for him; a new hand-knitted sweater and green canvas shoes imported from China.

She leant down to talk to him for a long time. With dark brown braids around her neck, she reassured him about the school he'd be going to, in a big city. She put on a brave front, telling her young son that it would exciting to see cars, planes, trucks, electric lights—all the things he'd always wanted to see—and make friends with other boys.

But Sanduk had no conception of what she was talking about. Walung was his whole world. 'My childish concern was really only of my precious collection of yak horns and special pebbles; I wanted to take my treasured keepsakes with me,' he recalls. 'So together we put them on a special shelf and she promised me she would not let anyone touch them until I returned.'

On the day Sanduk left, his mother gave him a small handmade bag she'd sewn out of the same red-and-white striped material her aprons were made out of. She'd sewn bells on the outside, and had filled it with flour biscuits, handmade chocolates and *churpi,* a type of sweet, hard cheese, and told him not to eat them all in one day.

As she leant down and put it around his neck, the enormity of what was happening began to sink in.

Butter lamps were lit in the windows of their home (a traditional Tibetan Buddhist ritual in which yak butter is burnt), incense was burnt, and his father started chanting prayers. Outside he could hear the yak bells clanging as his father's small caravan prepared to leave the village.

Sanduk pressed himself into his mother's woollen tunic, inhaling the familiar smell of yak wool, wood smoke and the spices she used to make tea. 'This is just something you have to do, my dear,' she told him, holding him close, and softly stroking his head. 'Be a very good boy. Do everything your teachers ask you. You're going to be looked after very well, and you'll be coming back soon.'

Sanduk shut his eyes, and wrapped his arms around his mother's waist, burying his head into her apron. His father gently pulled Sanduk away and nudged him toward the stone path heading out of the gorge, away from the village and everything he knew to be safe and familiar. They joined the caravan and headed toward the thunderous torrent of the Tamor River.

He was seven years old.

He looked back several times. As their party descended the path, Kasang was standing clutching her apron, her face streaked with tears. Neither of them knew it at the time, but he would not see her again for three years.

2

VERTIGO

'Slow your pace down to that of the yaks,' Sonam told his young son as they navigated the narrow mountain passes, their backs pressed against the cliff faces. 'And look where you are going. Don't put your foot down unless you've worked out what stone or rock you are going to land on. Don't look down, don't look around, and don't get distracted.' It was good advice for the journey of life.

The Himalayas have long been romanticised as a place of rugged and luminous beauty. The explorer and writer Peter Matthiessen, one of the first Westerners to enter Tibet via Nepal, seems to have fallen under a kind of spell when he first saw Mount Everest, describing it in his 1978 book *The Snow Leopard* as 'glistening like a spire of a higher kingdom'.

As a boy, Sanduk was taught to regard the mountains, especially Kanchenjunga, their home mountain, as a place of sacred power. Rather than something to conquer, in the view of many Westerners, the mountains were a place that commanded great respect, calling upon great reserves of fortitude, faith and physical strength simply to survive.

Now Sanduk was about to find out himself just how dangerous crossing the roof of the world could be. In a trip that would be almost unimaginable to most boys of the same age, Sanduk walked with his father for two weeks in his simple Chinese sneakers across stone crags, ice crusts, and over torrential rivers on flimsy log bridges.

Their destination was St Robert's School, a Jesuit boarding school his father had enrolled him into at Darjeeling, West Bengal, in northern India. The trip was probably about 150 kilometres as the crow flies, but the path was so rocky and winding that the real distance is impossible to measure. At that time, there was no other way to get there.

His father walked along the narrow ledges and stone paths as if it was second nature; he was as nimble and sure-footed as the yaks. Elegant even. But at seven, Sanduk was still finding his feet. There were many moments in those first hard days when he stumbled, or tripped, or was so terrified that his feet refused to budge. It was then that Sonam's loyal assistant, Dharkey, who helped him with everything from arranging trips to his business affairs, would coax the boy onwards.

Sanduk trusted Dharkey. 'He had such a kind face. He would hold my hand crossing the roads and bridges that I was frightened by and would pat me to sleep at night. He'd help me put my coat on and make sure I'd eaten enough breakfast before I started out.'

On the first night, Sonam and Dharkey were too exhausted to cook anything other than porridge with dried meat. Sanduk was on the verge of tears; he desperately wanted to go back home, back to his mother's kitchen and his warm bed by the fire with all his family.

'I must have been anxious, sleeping in a cave in the mountains, because when I woke up in the morning, I realised I'd peed into the sheepskin rug I'd been sleeping on.'

His father, normally so strict, must have understood how strange all this was for the seven-year-old. As they watched the sun light up the south face of Kanchenjunga, Sonam simply brewed tea, made porridge, and threw the sodden blanket on the back of a yak to dry in the sun. Nothing was ever said about the matter.

Sanduk dreaded every one of the small, swaying suspension bridges that punctuated their journey. One step in the wrong direction and he could fall into the crevasse. Mistakes could be fatal. At one point, they crossed the roaring Tamor River on a single plank of wood.

'I remember that Dharkey held one of my hands, and another trader held the other. I didn't look down. I knew if I'd fallen into the river, I would have just been swept away.'

Sanduk's strength grew quickly; within days he realised he was made of the same stuff as his father. Toward the end, he took pride in keeping up with everyone else in the party.

Often, he would walk in his father's or Dharkey's footsteps for hours. He remembers listening to the fast thud of his own heart and using every muscle in his body to keep up with the men.

He grew fond of the yaks with their fluffy tails; how nimble they were at high altitudes above the snowline, and how they slowed down and grew stubborn at the lower altitudes. He loved the brightly coloured ribbons and bells tied to their woolly manes.

They had that barren, awe-inspiring landscape all to

themselves. They didn't meet anyone else for the entire trip. It was just snow, rock and sky. The only sounds were the swoosh of eagles overhead, the roar of the river, and the occasional rockslide. Sometimes it was so quiet that the silence seemed to ping. At night, they would camp in shepherds' huts or caves that Sonam or Dharkey knew from their many previous trips. They would make a small fire and cook corn and potatoes, or *dal bhat*.

At night, the stars were so bright and close that Sanduk felt as if he could reach out and touch them. He would fall asleep as soon as he lay his head on the blankets Dharkey had laid down for him.

The most gruelling part was along the border of eastern Nepal and India. They were on an exposed ridge for days, in a blizzard, with the sub-zero wind and snow whipping around them from every direction. Sanduk had a cap, but no gloves, and his fingers were so cold they felt as if they were going to snap off. The wind seemed to pierce through his clothes and lash his body. It almost took his breath away.

Sonam's party only began to thaw out as they descended out of this stone and ice world and into the softer, gentler foothills around West Bengal, near Darjeeling. Suddenly, within an hour, it seemed, they emerged into a completely different landscape. They made their way through forests of juniper and oak trees and banks of rhododendrons, and his father pointed out the bamboo thickets that were home to the elusive red pandas. Sanduk was mesmerised by the rich colours; the yellow corn fields and the velvety green tea gardens, stretching out around them, as far as they could see.

On the last day of the trek, when Sanduk and Sonam emerged into the outskirts of Darjeeling, his senses were overwhelmed by the noise and mayhem.

Swarms of bicycles buzzed by, their bells jangling like a chorus. Radios blared Hindu music from shops, their shelves loaded with glass jars filled with lollies and biscuits. The women looked like exotic creatures, wearing colourful saris and daubs of red paint on their foreheads. Even more astonishing were the tall Caucasians with their blue eyes and blond hair.

It was the first time Sanduk had ever laid eyes on a bus. 'I thought they were a very curious looking machine,' he says. It helped that they were decorated that day, as they are so often in India and Nepal, with garlands of marigold flowers to celebrate one of the Hindu community's many holy days.

As Sanduk stood there trying to take in the chaotic pageant, an overpowering sense of inferiority swept over him.

'I remember looking down at my own clothes and feeling so embarrassed by my homespun yak wool trousers and shirt. I felt like such a country hick. It was as if I'd somehow turned up in a modern city from prehistoric times. I wanted to disappear, or hide.'

He didn't get a chance. The next thing Sanduk knew, his father was bidding farewell to Dharkey and the rest of the group, and wrangling his son up onto the roof of one of the buses. 'I remember staring at its large rubber wheels in amazement. Was this thing going to fly? Was a horse going to drag it along? Was it going to float on water?' He got some of the other passengers to help us find a seat on the roof. The noise coming out of it as the driver turned a handle at the

front and the engine started gave me such a fright. I remember
Dad holding me close to him as we bumped our way over the
road and around the bends.'

When the bus finally shuddered to a halt at Darjeeling, with
a blast of black soot, they clambered off and walked through
the town, along the high ridge with views of the Himalayas,
to St Robert's School, a solid brick residence built by British
missionaries in the 1930s. Sanduk was limping from blisters
as they crossed the lawn. Neither he nor his father said a
word as they looked up at the large wooden doors. They
knocked and took a deep breath.

20

3

HEY, BHOTEY

The boarding school Sonam had chosen for his son did not enjoy the picturesque grandeur of nearby St Joseph's School which, with its handsome sandstone buildings, was framed by the snow-capped Himalayas. St Robert's, by comparison, was a run-of-the-mill, government-funded school costing about $14 a year for boarding and tuition. 'It was the equivalent of two yaks, or six months' salary,' Sanduk says. 'St Robert's was one of the most affordable schools in Darjeeling, but for my parents it was quite a lot of money at the time.'

The 300 students who trooped into the three-storey building with a plain tin roof were mainly from India's lower and middle class.

The warden at the time, a Jesuit priest called Father William Mackey, peered down from under a thatch of snowy white hair at the seven-year-old standing before him in his homespun clothes. The curiosity was mutual. Sanduk looked up at the tall man with cobalt blue eyes, wearing what seemed to be a dress, a garment that turned out to be a clergyman's cloak. 'I remember Father Mackey gave me a funny little smile . . . it was as if he'd known me for a long time.' Little did Sanduk know what a comfort Father Mackey's friendship would be to him during the next six years.

Everything at the school, even the most common objects, were totally unfamiliar to Sanduk. The tables, the chairs, the blackboards, the electric lights, the radio and the heaters— he'd never seen any such things before. He stood with his mouth open, taking it all in. After a tour of the school grounds, he was taken to the tailor, where he was measured up for his uniform of grey pants, grey sweater and white shirt, all of which made him feel even more ill-at-ease.

Sanduk was just as taken aback when he was shown the boarding house, a separate residence not far from the school, where he was to live for the next six years.

It was originally built in the 1930s when the British had turned Darjeeling into a genteel hill station for the colonial administration. Its wide wooden stairs ran elegantly between the two storeys, and the surrounding lawns and gardens were meant to be reminiscent of the English countryside.

He was shown the room he was to sleep in, filled with about eight narrow wooden bunks. For someone used to sleeping around the embers of the fire on a mattress with his family close by, the arrangement must have seemed decidedly odd.

'Were you supposed to sleep on the top bunk one night, and the bottom the second? I was scratching my head, trying to work out how these double-bunkers worked.'

Sonam placed his son's small metal trunk filled with special quilts his mother had sewn for him on top of his bunk. Sanduk was unpacking them, getting his bearings, when his father said something he couldn't understand at all at first. He squatted down on his haunches beside Sanduk, put his hands on his shoulders, and said, 'Son, I have to leave you now. You need to be a good boy. Study hard, read everything you can, and I'll come back soon.'

Sanduk was incredulous. His father was going to leave him alone in this strange place, surrounded by strange people? 'My father had always been a fairly distant, authoritarian figure, but suddenly I realised how important he was to me. I remember clinging to him and saying, "I don't want to stay here! Not on my own!" I remember him stroking my head, and trying to comfort me. He kept saying, "You're going to be okay, my boy. You'll be okay. They'll look after you well, and I'll come back soon." He promised to come back at the first school holiday.'

Sonam gave his son a long firm hug and walked away. As Sanduk stared at his big hat and tall frame filling the doorway, every fibre of him wanted to run and throw his arms around his father. But the trek had changed him. He knew his father would be ashamed of him if he seemed so afraid, so he stood stock-still beside his bunk. Sonam turned around, gave him a long, lingering look, as if he was trying to memorise his son's face, then walked away.

Sanduk didn't want anyone to see him crying, so he sat down in a corner and put his head in his hands. He got the red-and-white bag his mother had given him and nibbled some of the biscuits and cheese she'd made, but it was of little consolation. He couldn't work out how he was going to get through the day.

Father Mackey found him. He reached down and held

Sanduk's hands, helped him stand up, and led him into the kitchen to make some tea. 'You're a very brave boy. You've come from far, far away.'

Father Mackey tried to cheer Sanduk up by pinching his cheeks, which were bright red, because of the altitude of Walung, and seemed to be able to tell instinctively when he was bereft with homesickness. 'His nickname for me was "Apples". He always kept an eye out for me.'

The worst part of boarding school were the holidays. Although his father promised to come back as soon as he could, it was three years before Sonam finally made it back to St Robert's. Until then, Sanduk was the only one left behind at the end of every term. He was told his parents weren't coming, because they were too far away, but he would sit in the corner as all the parents arrived, and forlornly stare at them collecting their children. He kept hoping, in his secret childish way, that one day someone would come for him.

When everyone had gone home, he would seek solace in the garden, crushed with disappointment and homesickness. He could see Mount Kanchenjunga from there and would try to imagine what his family was doing. His mother would probably be spinning yak wool, and his father would be preparing for another trek into Tibet for salt. His sisters and brother would be playing by the river. He'd fantasise about his homecoming.

Father Mackey was always sensitive to how desperately lonely Sanduk was feeling and would give him tasks to distract him.

'He'd ask me to sort out a stack of books, or water the garden, or chop up vegetables for dinner. He took me for long strolls through Darjeeling. We spent hours inside the

Himalayan Mountaineering Institute, learning about Tenzing Norgay, the first Nepalese to summit Mount Everest. We went to the zoo, and looked at the snow leopard, the red pandas and black bears. He gave me my first real instructions about politics—trying to explain why India and China were fighting. I'll never forget the time and attention he gave me.'

He also showed Sanduk the library at St Robert's, the door to other worlds. He had that treasure trove to himself for weeks at a time. He would close the door and pore over maps of the world for hours, and sit enthralled reading stories about great explorers such as Marco Polo.

Father Mackey told Sanduk, 'It's very important that you read, Sanduk. And it's important that you remember what you read. And that you apply what you remember.'

Father Mackey was the first of a series of father figures for Sanduk. He loved the richness of friendship with someone older than himself, someone who could impart wisdom, and who had so much to offer. He felt he had so much to learn. The only language Sanduk spoke when he arrived at St Robert's was a Tibetan-style dialect spoken by the tribes who lived around Kanchenjunga. At first, the lessons meant nothing to him as he knew neither Nepali nor English. 'I remember sitting up the back, scratching my head, not understanding a word anyone was saying. I was close to tears. I felt so small. I'd put my head in my hands. Everything just looked like strange squiggles on the page. I didn't talk to anyone. I had absolutely no confidence at all.' As usual, Father Mackey tried to make things easier. He gave Sanduk some books meant for younger children that were a lot simpler to read.

It was six months before the squiggles on the page began to rearrange themselves into recognisable letters, and for the letters to become words, and finally for the words to become sentences. Seven months after he'd arrived, he could understand most things the teachers were saying in Nepali, and even raise his hand in class and ask a few questions. By the end of the first year, he was doing extremely well. Despite being a relatively inexpensive school, the curriculum first established by the 16th Jesuit, Ignatius of Loyola, meant Sanduk received a thorough education.

Sanduk rose at 6 a.m. for physical exercises, followed by lessons all day: French, Latin, English, maths, geography and history. Bells punctuated the day—bells to start lunch and bells to finish, a bell for dinner and a bell for bedtime.

Father Mackey never discussed his own religion. Instead, he asked Sanduk about his family's Buddhist faith. 'He never tried to convert me to Christianity, which I respected him for. I remember the hymns on Sunday morning in the high-ceilinged chapel, and how everything seemed so clean and bright. There were crucifixes and scripts of the Bible on the walls throughout the school grounds. The priest would give me confession, and I tried communion a few times, kneeling at the altar and taking the wafer representing Christ's body.'

All this meant little to Sanduk, but he admired their belief and their sincerity. No matter how kind Father Mackay was, however, Sanduk was bullied at school. He was called *bhotey*, meaning country bumpkin. He would be given a big hard whack on the back of his head, and have his woollen jumper yanked off. 'No-one comes to take you home in the holidays, do they, hey, *bhotey*?' the bullies taunted.

The shy country boy was an easy target. He found it a strain to sit up straight at the dining table, let alone use a knife and a fork. He was used to the river and rhododendrons. Instead he was surrounded by concrete buildings, paved roads and timetables. He put his head down, fell into line, followed the rules, spoke to no-one for a month, and hugged his misery to himself like one of his father's thick sheepskin jackets.

During one of the holidays in his third year, Sanduk hit an all-time low. He developed a fever which became so bad that he had abscesses on his buttocks. It was excruciatingly painful. He couldn't lie down, he couldn't sit, nor could he walk. All the teachers and students were away on holiday, even Father Mackey. The only person living at the hostel at the time was the cook, who took him to the civil hospital in Darjeeling.

Sanduk was horrified by what he saw. 'There were patients lying in dirty sheets, people sitting on mattresses on the floor in the corridor waiting to see a doctor. There didn't seem to be enough sheets, or blankets, or beds, let alone equipment, or staff. They found a bed for me, and put me on antibiotics.'

Before the drugs kicked in, Sanduk taught himself to control the pain by counting. As the pain peaked, he would count to ten and hold his breath. As it subsided, he would breathe out again.

The operation was crude. He had a local anaesthetic, but the nerves were exposed. He shuddered and cried out with pain as hands held him down while the pus was removed. The recovery was agonising as well. Every day he had to have a sitz bath, a warm shallow bath filled with potassium permanganate, a salt solution used to treat infections. He learnt to manage the pain by clenching his fists, and when it became almost unbearable, squeezing his eyes shut.

Sanduk was in hospital for three weeks but time went so slowly that it felt more like three years. He longed for his mother and dreamed of her at night. Sometimes she seemed so real that it was as if she was standing by his bed, gazing at him with calm maternal love. He felt he could almost reach out and touch her red woollen tunic.

He still can't remember one friendly face during his stay there. He would look to the nurses for reassurance or sympathy but was met with only harried glances. 'They weren't unkind, they were just understaffed, just run off their feet.'

Those weeks in hospital gave Sanduk a mental strength he never lost. 'I realised that for someone like me, nothing was ever going to just land in my lap. I had no money, and no connections. Life was going to be a struggle. But I was smart. And determined. I could work hard, very hard. I vowed to myself that once I'd got through this pain and out of this hospital I was going to fight hard for a good life.'

If Kasang couldn't come to him, he was determined to mend as fast as he could, build up his strength and go to her instead. Going home was an all-consuming goal.

During his time at St Robert's, his worst affliction was homesickness. He tried to fight off the bouts by joining the soccer team, attempting to distract himself with the rough camaraderie of his teammates. He did eventually go home once during his six years at boarding school—but, sadly, it was not to Walung. Shortly after he set off for the two-week journey home, accompanied by Dharkey, by truck, then on foot, he was given the bad news:the Tamor River had flooded the gorge, washing away several of the houses and damaging many, including Sanduk's family home. With the trade route into Tibet now closed, it seemed futile to the villagers to rebuild Walung.

Sonam and Kasang, like most of the other inhabitants, salvaged their belongings, and decided to try their luck by heading down out of the mountains, south-west to the large trading town of Dhankuta. His parents started again, buying a piece of land and a small house in the little village of Hille on the outskirts, pretty enough to be called 'The Darjeeling of Nepal'. They rolled up their sleeves, got to work, and rebuilt their lives as shopkeepers, selling clothes and medicinal herbs.

It was a big adjustment for Sonam to give up his life as a wayfaring trader; he loved being outdoors with the sun on his face, travelling across the mountains where he knew every rock, every stone, and every bend in the path. But he dealt with the loss with the stoicism the Himalayan people are renowned for. The harshness of the landscape and their lives forced the Walunga tribe to accept hardship as inevitable and just keep going. Head down, one foot in front of the other— that's how they survived. Sonam and Kasang had a roof over their head. They had a livelihood. And they had five healthy children. There was much to be thankful for.

After three years away, Sanduk was in a storm of impatience to see his family again.

'I can't remember how many days it took Dharkey and me to get to Hille, maybe thirteen days or so. We seemed to walk through the tea gardens and through juniper forests forever. Each day, and each hour, I got more and more excited about going home and seeing my mother again.'

When Sonam and Kasang heard via the postman and travellers passing through the region that Sanduk and Dharkey were almost home, they sent a boy with hot milk and biscuits to greet them, as was the custom. Night was falling as Sanduk and Dharkey finally approached the small settlement of Hille. 'It's difficult to describe the feeling other than this overwhelming excitement. I could not think of anything else except my mother's face. There was nothing else in my mind.'

Kasang was standing on the doorway, waiting for him. She gave her son a big hug and held him tightly. 'Oh, you've grown so tall! And you're so thin!'

She'd made a special meal of dumplings, sweet cheese and biscuits. All of Sanduk's aunts, uncles and family crowded into the room to see how much he'd grown and to hear all about school. He stayed with his family for three weeks, stealing apricots and apples from farmers' fields with his friends. He revelled in all the comforts of home, sitting by the fire at night, watching his mother knit and gossip with his aunties, and enjoying Kasang's homemade food. He and Yangla spent days by the river where she quizzed him about his life in Darjeeling. 'She wanted to know everything about boarding school—what I ate, where I slept, whether I'd seen movies, what the big city was like. What the other boys were like. And she sang a lot. I always loved listening to her beautiful singing.' It was a terrible wrench to leave and return to St Robert's.

Boarding school came to an abrupt end three years later, when Sanduk was thirteen years old. Sonam suddenly appeared at the dormitory one morning. The fighting between India and China had become so dangerous that the government had requested that the school be evacuated.

Sonam had come to fetch his son and bring him back to their new home in Hille. Within half an hour, Sanduk had packed his trunk and was saying goodbye to all his friends. Father Mackey, Sanduk's advocate to the very last minute, left his father with firm parting words.

'Make sure you continue his education,' he said. 'This boy will do something good in the future.'

4

YANGLA'S SONG

After he'd moved back to Hille from boarding school, Sanduk was not surprised to find his parents' business prospering. The Himalayan people are exceptionally good traders. With no other way to make a living, trading was a skill they'd mastered, and which was passed down the generations from father to son. They're thrifty, too. If the family earns ten rupees, they would spend four and save six. Sanduk's cousin Tenzing Ukyab recalls, 'That adds up over the years and the family would have a tidy bundle to tide over rough times. They made good investments in gold, silver and jewellery. Sonam was always a good businessman, he was very smart, very enterprising.'

The couple's three daughters, Yangla, Chhengjing and Chundak, were thriving in their new home in the hills among the orange trees, bamboo and marigold flowers.

Sonam began preparing to send his second son Ladenla to boarding school.

Although Sanduk fervently wished to continue his education, he was never to return to St Robert's in Darjeeling. His heart sank when his father told him he had enrolled his son at the Siddhartha Vanasthali School in Kathmandu. It was 400 kilometres away—almost twice as far as Darjeeling. Sanduk had learned through bitter experience that homesickness was more a physical sensation than an emotional one. All too often, he would feel he was sinking under waves of nausea. He'd have knots in his stomach, and no appetite for days. He was only free from its grip when he had a chance to go home, something that happened far too rarely for his liking—usually once a year.

There were frequent bouts of dysentery to endure as well as he settled into the school's dingy hostel, where he would share a dorm with five or six other students. 'The food was lousy, really terrible: rice and very thin dhal, and the same curry every time. I remember I used to sit for hours under a big tree outside the school feeling really unwell.'

But St Robert's had toughened him up. By the time he'd arrived at the Siddhartha Vanasthali School, Sanduk was fluent in Nepali, had reasonably good English, and had a flair for biology, literature and history. 'I'd begun to enjoy the feeling of doing well,' he says. He also knew that completing high school might open the door for him to study at university, something nobody in his family or village had ever considered possible. He put his head down and studied like a demon.

By the time he was in high school, Sanduk was light years away from the mischievous village boy he'd once been. He was a conscientious student. He had an iron will to get ahead in life and make his mark on the world.

A relative let him stay in his run-down old flat on the outskirts of the city. It was just one room and a kitchen, and there was no electricity. He studied by candlelight, long into the night, every night. He was determined to win a scholarship to a prestigious university. He peddled the long distance from the flat to school on a shoddy second-hand bicycle.

Ukyab noticed how focused his cousin had become. He seemed to know exactly what he wanted to do. 'I knew even back then, that he would achieve what he was after.'

While Sanduk was away at high school in Kathmandu, two dramatic events occurred that would change his life. Several years into his education, Sonam and Kesang suffered another devastating blow. Their youngest daughter Chundak developed a severe fever and died. She was eight years old. Although Sanduk hardly knew his little sister, he had watched his mother's pride as her rosy-cheeked daughter helped her around the home. His parents had already lost their first son, before he was born, and now they had lost a daughter as well.

Returning home to Hille during his school holiday shortly after Chundak's death, Sanduk watched with quiet desperation at the way it changed his parents. Sonam, always a man of few words, refused to speak about it at all. But Sanduk noticed the deep worry lines that had etched his forehead. He suddenly looked a decade older. As for Kasang, the loss also aged her dramatically as well. She continued looking after the rest of the family, but to Sanduk, she seemed to have shrunk under the weight of her sorrow. She seemed shorter, and was rail thin. Sanduk felt his parents' anguish keenly.

'Child mortality rates were high at that time in countries like Nepal, about 25 to 30 per cent, but that didn't stop the heartache,' Sanduk says. 'It was part of life at that time in Nepal. But I knew they must have been really heartbroken.

35

As a father, I can't imagine anything worse. There's nothing parents dread more than losing their own children.'

No-one could have guessed there was worse to come. During Sanduk's last year of high school, Sonam enrolled fifteen-year-old Yangla in a girls' school not far from his, the Mahendra Bhawan Higher Secondary School. Yangla moved in with him and they soon created a special little world of their own.

Her sweet demeanour and beautiful brown eyes fringed with dark lashes were like a balm after Sanduk's six years of austerity at boarding school. He treasured every moment of domestic comfort. She would place a blanket over him when he was falling asleep, and after every meal, she would ask her brother, 'Have you eaten enough?'

He would buy the groceries and Yangla would cook. They went out to the movies. Their prized possession was a transistor radio, and Yangla would sing as she'd cook, often to Nepali love songs by the likes of Aruna Lama. The flat was filled with her melodious voice.

When Sanduk had examinations, she'd wake him up early with cups of *chia*, the sweet Nepalese tea brewed with cardamom, cloves, cinnamon, milk and sugar. 'She'd say to me, "Brother, brother, you have to get up and study!" She was so proud of how well I was doing. They were such happy times.'

For a year, their lives seemed to gleam with possibilities. Yangla was studying as hard as her brother. They dreamed about their futures: Yangla as a teacher, and Sanduk as a pilot or businessman. Yangla had admirers who wanted to ask her out, so Sanduk kept a protective, brotherly eye on her.

But in the second year of school, Yangla started losing weight. Fast. No matter how much she ate, she couldn't seem to put it back on again. She was always coughing. Sanduk wrote a letter to his parents in Hille. Sonam came to Kathmandu as soon as he could, and they took her to two different hospitals. The doctors examined her skin, her phlegm, and gave her an X-ray. The tests confirmed their worst fears. She had tuberculosis.

Yangla was taken to a sanatorium up in the hills, about 10 kilometres out of Kathmandu. Sanduk used to cycle there every couple of days, and Yangla would always be sitting up in bed, looking out the window, waiting for him. They had long talks about life, and their family and friends. Within weeks, she started coming good. She put on weight. Her eyes were bright. She started singing her favourite songs softly under her breath.

She even began working in the family's shop in Hille, charming the customers with her pretty face. But just when they all thought she was out of danger, she started losing weight again. This time it just fell off her already bird-like frame.

Their nearest hospital, in Dhankuta, was run by the British Nepal Medical Trust and they told the Ruit family that Yangla would probably need a second line of treatment. To their anguish, the medicine was too expensive and too hard to obtain. 'Even if we'd sold everything we could, we still wouldn't have been able to afford that medicine.'

There was an unsaid expectation that as the elder brother with the most education, Sanduk would be the one most likely to be able to save her. But he was only eighteen years old. He didn't have any medical connections yet, nor any money. He would never feel so helpless again in his life. He wanted to scoop her up into his arms and knock on every door for help. He would have changed places with her in an instant.

'It was horrific, watching her slip away from us, knowing the drugs that would have saved her were unobtainable to us. To hear the doctor say "We can't do much about her, so maybe you should take her home" was one of the worst moments of my life. I wanted it to be me, not her.'

The last time Sanduk ever saw Yangla, she was in their parents' shop, trying valiantly to sell clothes. She had become so thin it was almost painful to look at her. Her eyes had become enormous as tuberculosis ravaged her slender figure.

'Her skin had gone very dark and she was speaking slowly. She tried to be cheerful but I think she was waiting for destiny; she had quietly accepted that she would not live for long. She was in a really bad way,' he recalls. She told her brother she just felt so tired, and there was nothing left to do.

One of the hardest things Ruit has ever had to do in his life was to go back to Kathmandu the next day to sit for his leaving certificate to graduate from high school. If he hadn't gone, he would have to wait an entire year to sit the same exam.

Sanduk held his sister's hands in his. 'She looked directly into my eyes and said, "I may not see you again, dear brother. Do good things in your life." It was a look of both resignation and lost hope. The desperate grip of her hands was unforgettable. It was as if she was clinging to life itself.' She was telling Sanduk, with her eyes, and with her grasp, with all the strength she had left in her, that he had to do something to help people like her, and that he had to do it *now*.

Somehow Sanduk managed to get up and walk out of that room where she lay dying, go home and pack his bags, and return to high school in Kathmandu. Yangla passed away a few days later. He walked around the school grounds in a daze. It seemed impossible to study. He was so restless, so agitated. His chest hurt. His throat ached. He couldn't concentrate. He found it hard to talk to anyone. It seemed futile to start anything. He was haunted by the image of Yangla looking up at him, calling him 'elder brother' and placing all her hopes in him.

'I kept thinking, *What if? What if we'd had enough money? What if we'd taken her to a doctor sooner? What if we'd known people who could help?*'

He couldn't listen to the radio. Every song reminded him of the way she used to sing. Schoolchildren in the street reminded him of the classes she would never teach.

He packed away her mattress and her clothes. He lay awake at night, tossing and turning, tormented by the thought that maybe Yangla could have been saved if they had known what to do, or had more money, or known more people in the right places.

Before Sanduk had turned nineteen, he had already lost half his family. His elder brother to diarrhoea before he was born, then his eight-year-old sister Chundak to fever, and now his beloved Yangla to tuberculosis. But unlike his father, Sanduk could not accept such tragedy as simply his lot in life. Stripped raw by shock and grief, it was as if a veil had lifted. What had happened suddenly seemed like a monumental injustice.

'It was not unusual for 50 per cent of your family members to die in Nepal. For most people, losing one out of four children was still considered normal fate. But suddenly, I simply could not understand, and I could not accept, that half my family had to die simply because we were poor and lived in a remote part of the world. Losing Yangla, as well as Chundak, would be something that time would never really heal. Our family got on with life, but we never recovered from it.'

He was infuriated that his siblings had died from diseases that were readily cured in the West. It suddenly seemed completely unacceptable. 'I think what did it was the final connection with my sister, that moment that she looked at me, that I knew exactly what I had to do.'

He had to be a doctor.

At the time, it was unheard of for someone from such a remote mountain village with no school to study medicine. Sonam, a man of iron will himself, was firmly against it. 'He just thought it was out of the box for someone from the Walung tribe. He wanted me to help him with the family business instead.'

But Yangla's death gave him courage and self-conviction. He put his head down and studied hard for a Colombo Plan scholarship, which uses foreign aid to pay for the university fees of the poorest but brightest Indian and Nepalese students. His aim: King George's Medical University in Lucknow, northern India, known as one of the 'Ivy League' universities of the subcontinent.

More than 150 students sat for the examination. Only eight were successful. When Sanduk received the news he'd been accepted, he didn't feel jubilant, or exultant, the way you do if you've kicked a goal in the grand final. 'I felt really calm. I knew I was on the right path. It was the first step I needed to take to make sure my brother and sisters had not died in vain.'

Yangla was cremated in Hille. There's no trace of her, save for one poignant photograph of her about the age of eight, sitting demurely on a rock in the sunshine. There is no necklace, no earrings or keepsake to remember her by. Her gift was to steer her elder brother toward becoming a doctor. Yangla may be out of sight, but she is not out of mind. Sanduk's love for her, as well as for Chundak, and his unknown brother, lives on in every patient he treats, every person he cares for.

5

THE GIFT

For most Nepalese, gaining an education usually means travelling far from home, and in 1972, when Ruit was eighteen, he set off to study medicine in the third largest city of northern India. For the next six years he was to live among more than one million people, more than 1000 kilometres from his family.

King George's Medical University was a world away from St Robert's School and the Siddhartha Vanasthali School; the term 'Ivy League' was used for good reason. Like many of the other buildings in Lucknow, King George's was an elaborate mixture of Indian and Victorian architecture. Its bright white pavilions, domes and scalloped arches, built in 1912, made it look more like a giant wedding cake than a campus. Ruit certainly found it intimidating. He felt sick with nerves as he crossed the emerald green lawn in his best clothes, carrying a small duffle bag from home.

His hostel room had space within the chalky white walls and high ceilings for a bed, a desk and all his textbooks.

His 200 colleagues, apart from a handful from Malaysia, were sons of India's upper class who went on to become the top specialists in India, the United Kingdom, the United States and Europe.

Ruit had competed with more than 150 of India and Nepal's brightest students to win a scholarship. He had just as much right to be there as everyone else. But as he sat down in the lectures of anatomy and physiology, biochemistry and pharmacology, he could not shake off the feeling of being an interloper. He was the son of a salt trader. He was an outsider.

He was one of the few Nepalese among a sea of Indian faces. Who was he to be there with the best and brightest of the subcontinent?

'I was painfully aware that I came from one of the lowest castes. I still felt very much like that country hick I'd been dubbed in boarding school. I looked different to the others—a little bit Mongoloid. The other students joshed about with each other, saying, "Hey, man," that sort of thing. But they didn't mix with me at all. They kept their distance.'

People often underestimated Ruit because he is quietly spoken. He downplays the caste system, but the reality was that the Sherpas and Walunga people were downtrodden by the higher castes, especially in a field like medicine. Ruit was determined to prove he could achieve things.

But first there was the practical matter of adjusting to the climate. For someone who had grown up in a village with sub-zero temperatures near the third highest mountain in the world, the monsoonal rains and scorching heat nearly knocked him sideways. Most days in summer the tempera-ture soared well above 40 degrees. 'I remember walking over the bridge over the Gomati River to my hostel, and I could see that the bitumen was actually literally *sizzling*,' he says.

Despite being an outsider, Ruit made a couple of good, close friends and on Saturday nights they would go out in a rickshaw and feast on kebabs and biryanis, the northern Indian delicacy of aromatic rice, finishing with *kulfi*, the city's famous frozen dessert, and see an English or a Hindi film. On the weekends, he would wend his way through the city's labyrinthine streets, staring in astonishment at the cornucopia of goods crammed into the city's shops; colourful kites, bolts of expensive muslin, loaves of bread, handmade sweets, and fresh roses and jasmine.

His familiar old nemesis, homesickness, turned up frequently. The post was slow between India and Nepal, and no-one in his family was a fluent writer, so often it was six months before he had news from home. During low moments, he would find consolation by strolling down to the river at sunset. Lucknow was famous for its grand palaces and tombs built during the Mogul empire, and one of the grandest of these was an 18th-century mosque, the Bara Imambara. Somehow, gazing at its ornate domes in the late afternoon light never failed to soothe him, and he would walk back to his studies with renewed vigour.

Besides, soon after arriving, Ruit gained something more important than popularity: his peers' grudging respect for his work ethic, particularly his ability to study through the night. Some of the students became resentful of his academic prowess.

Like most of the first-year students, he had any squeamishness knocked out of him by learning how to dissect a cadaver.

'My God, the smell!' he says, recalling the overpowering smell of formaldehyde as he walked into the dissection room.

Four students were assigned to each body. He remembers the way the room spun about him; and that he had to hold onto a bench to stop himself from passing out when he approached the body he'd been assigned to. Ruit's task was to dissect the thorax, the flesh at the front of the chest, which seemed to be still pulsing with blood and nerves. His hands trembled when he picked up the knife and gingerly poked at the flesh. He couldn't stop thinking about the man lying before him on the cold steel table. How many children did he have? Who had loved him and who had he loved? How had he died? He was shrunken and dark, and Ruit guessed he might have been a rickshaw driver. He had to take a shower after each session to wash off his revulsion.

But within weeks, 'surgery on dead people', as he called it, became a routine part of the week. He had become desensitised to the process. After a while, it didn't feel like he was cutting into a person. It was simply a piece of flesh on which he needed to learn how to skilfully wield his surgeon's knife. The same process happened with the skeleton in a box assigned to each new student that they were expected to keep in their hostel room. The first night, his skeleton kept him awake for hours; at 3 a.m. he admitted defeat, got up, pushed the box outside his door and went back to bed. The next week he brought the box back in. 'By the end of the semester, I was stashing peanuts in the eye sockets.'

One thing was patently clear: the boy from the backblocks had an uncanny gift for surgery. One of his first examinations involved being able to dissect one of the walls of a pelvic cavity within 45 minutes. He had to identify and display all the parts immaculately as he went along, painting the arteries red, and the veins blue. He was working away furiously, completely absorbed in the task, and when he looked up he realised he'd beaten everyone else by almost ten minutes, without making one mistake. He had won the university's gold medal for dissection. It was the first time in his life he had truly excelled at something. It was one of the happiest days of his university life.

After that, he blazed his way through his medical degree. He stayed up late, night after night studying, memorising the textbooks. 'There were many dawns when I woke up and found I'd fallen asleep over my textbook. My desk was my bed.'

It was a period of great intellectual curiosity. He was enthralled by the mechanics of anatomy, as his understanding deepened of the genius of the human body. 'Once you see how it works, you begin to have enormous respect for the delicacy and strength of human tissue.'

The lectures were in English and Ruit was now much more proficient, thanks to his voracious appetite for *Reader's Digest*, and any other English magazines he could get his hands on, and an eight-month stint at the reception desk of Hotel Annapurna, a large, four-star tourist hotel in Kathmandu before he went to university.

He began as a bell boy at the hotel. Within a month, his vocabulary had expanded rapidly, alongside his ability to converse with foreigners from every level of society. His work ethic and impeccable manners were noticed by management, and he was asked to work at the front desk of the foyer. 'It was the very best way to learn English,' he says. 'I knew instinctively I would need to be fluent, and the hotel was jostling with foreigners—British, American, Canadian—all expecting excellent service. My job was to speak to them and make them feel at ease. I started with basic phrases like "Have a nice day" and "Where are you from?" and "Can I do anything to help?" I enjoyed learning to understand all the different accents, and the different characteristics, too. The British were so systematic and softly spoken and had such style, and the Americans were so outgoing and enthusiastic. I admired all of them, I sort of had stars in my eyes. I would try to emulate them when I spoke English.'

The graduation ceremony for Sanduk's medical degree in 1978, in the great hall of King George's, was a momentous day for his peers. Sanduk joined them as they filed up one by one to the stage to collect their medical degree in their traditional academic robes and caps. For him, though, it was just an ordinary day. He knew the 1000-kilometre trip to witness the ceremony would have been out of the question for his parents. 'Everyone else's family came except mine. I wasn't sad. I was expecting it.'

His years at boarding school had made him stoic.

'I'd become completely used to the fact that I had no family nearby. They lived too far away to be there, and it would have involved taking too much time out of my dad's trading schedule,' he says. Still, the importance of his degree, and his graduation day, did not escape him. The death of Yangla, Chundak and his older brother had brought about a clear-sighted vision that being a doctor was what he was put here on earth to do. To realise he had a physical gift as a surgeon was thrilling.

~

There were few accolades at Ruit's first job as a junior medical officer at Bir Hospital, the general hospital in Kathmandu. He started on the bottom rung, and was rotated from one chaotic department to another every couple of months. They were long days, and the work was tough. In the operating theatre, his role was to hold the retractors, the metal instruments used to separate the edges of the surgeon's incisions. If he didn't hold them properly, the senior doctors would slap his hand, or yell at him.

But it was a prestigious position for a boy from a remote mountain village. It was almost unheard of at the time for someone with no connections, from the Walunga tribe, to be working as a doctor in Nepal's busiest hospital. Sanduk rented a tiny apartment, and fuelled up for his long shifts in the hospital at the small cafe across the road every morning with a plate of fried rice and a cup of tea. He missed his family acutely—they were still in Hille, more than 400 kilometres away, a journey that took days by bus on the serpentine, mountainous roads. But his head was held high as he walked to work every morning as a fully-fledged doctor. 'I had an extreme sense of accomplishment when I first arrived at Kathmandu as a doctor. I really felt like I was on top of the world. There was even a slight sense of "Look at me now!", you know?' His father Sonam finally stopped cajoling him to join the family business. He began acknowledging his son's medical career was a rather fine thing, a feather in the cap, in fact, for the Ruit family.

Within months, Ruit's talents as a doctor began to shine. He was sent back to several rural villages, including his boyhood village, Walung, as the doctor for a government team surveying the border of Nepal and China. He saved several lives including a four-year-old boy who was close to death with gastroenteritis. The revival of the boy created a sensation in the village. Sanduk was flooded with a sense of elation.

'It felt so good, just so good, to come back to this place where I was born. This was where I had lost my elder brother, and here I was back again, saving a life. I remembered the strong grip of my sister. I remember feeling her presence very strongly and thinking, *Yes, Yangla, you're right, this really is what I was meant to be doing.*'

Working on the survey forced him to become painfully aware of the chronic need of medical care in Nepal's rural villages. 'I was able to look very closely at the ways of life of people. I saw the neglect, the poverty, how downtrodden they were.' He knew he would never be able to turn away from the suffering.

Ruit's watershed moment happened when he was asked to join the ophthalmology department, and he went with them on one of their outreach surgical camps.

In Nepal, like other developing countries, many people in remote or rural areas were simply unable to travel to city hospitals or clinics to have their eyes fixed. Often, they couldn't afford the bus fare, or were unable to take a week or two away from work. They were mainly farmers scratching out a living on the terraced hills and mountains. Unable to afford cars or motorbikes, they walked everywhere. They often went without basic necessities, such as paracetamol, antibiotics and soap.

So, the ophthalmology department would go out to them instead, packing up a small travelling surgery into a bus or a truck, and after travelling several hundred kilometres would set up a makeshift field hospital wherever they could—an old schoolroom, a clinic or monastery.

For Ruit, it was to be a week in which he felt as if he observed medical miracles. More than 300 blind people shuffled down mountain trails to the clinic in the foothills of the Annapurna range, holding onto the back of a relative's shirt tail, or holding their hand. They jostled to get to the screening table, clamouring for the chance for an operation and to see their loved ones again.

In 1980, a survey on blindness in the country had shown that 0.8 per cent of the population in Nepal were blind—not just visually impaired, but completely blind. That's about half a million people. What staggered Ruit was that 4 per cent of those cases had been caused by botched cataract surgery.

The cataracts in their eyes had paralysed them. The unlucky hand that fate had dealt them was to stay at home, often on their bed, totally dependent on their family. Because every family member contributes to the household's welfare in Nepal, blindness is a cruel blow.

The blind have to rely on another family member—usually the youngest daughter—to cook for them, dress them, lead them out into the sunshine for a walk, and take them to the toilet. Their carer usually had to leave school or work. So, one blind person removed two people from being involved in their community. They were treated with as much care as their family could give—but sometimes, some of them were treated worse than animals. 'I saw some cases that really shocked me,' Ruit says.

Often, the blind were malnourished, and the social isolation and lack of exercise made them susceptible to diseases, as well as depression.

'It's been proved several times that the life expectancy of people who are blind is shortened by at least 20 per cent, often more,' Ruit explains. 'The lack of authority in the family, and the loneliness, also makes it worse. Blind children in the developing world have a life expectancy of about five years.'

Some of them had walked for days to get to the camp; many had been lugged down along the mountain paths in basket taxis or carried in relative's arms or supported by them.

It was here that Ruit first did eye surgery, under the gaze of a senior surgeon. 'It was very difficult. I was very clumsy. I must admit I found it nice to watch but difficult to do. We worked like crazy, operating on more than 90 patients, finishing late in the night.'

Over the next few days, he helped unwrap many of their bandages and fitted patients with thick glasses, and got his first taste of the magic of restoring sight.

'Watching a blind person see again, become part of the visual world again, was so deeply moving,' he says. 'I'll never forget a family of five who were all blind, and as we watched them make their way back home, this time on their own, I realised that when you give people in these places their sight back, you give them their very *life* back. The eye is such a small organ, but it plays such an important role in a person's life.'

Ruit had found his mission in life. When he heard that the World Health Organization was offering a scholarship for an ophthalmic postgraduate degree in India, he used every ounce of his determination to win it.

He sailed his way through the examination. Armed with a recommendation from Dr Ram Pokhrel, the head of the Nepal Eye Hospital, and a senior director at the World Health Organization, the scholarship was his. The normally bolted door into the elite world of ophthalmology was opened for the talented young doctor from the border of Tibet.

What his medical colleagues might not have been aware of was that just as his career was beginning to take flight, Ruit was nursing a private heartache.

After living so far away in northern India for six years, Ruit was looking forward to seeing more of his family. Instead, he was shocked to discover a dramatic change in his younger brother, Ladenla.

Ladenla, as bright as his elder brother, brimming with potential, was dispatched to a prestigious boarding school in Darjeeling. But away from home, he'd fallen in with the wrong crowd and had become addicted to hard drugs.

Like the rest of the family, Ruit desperately wanted his brother to have self-respect, to be responsible, and to uphold the family name. They could only watch helplessly on the sidelines as he changed into someone who was tired and unreliable, and unable to hold down a regular job.

Ladenla stayed in Ruit's tiny Kathmandu flat for weeks at a time, and sometimes with his friends. For Ruit, it was like living with a complete stranger.

'My head was spinning. We loved him so much, but none of us knew what to do, how to help him.'

It was a painful time for the whole family, who did everything they could to help him overcome his addiction. They took him first to the doctor, then a rehabilitation centre in Kathmandu.

As the elder brother, and the doctor in the family, the responsibility fell heavily on Ruit to steer his brother back on track. But for the time being, he had to try and keep tabs on his brother from afar.

He was bound for the All India Institute of Medical Science (AIIMS) in New Delhi, India.

With its cutting-edge technology, extensive research library and public hospital that treated millions of people a year for a low cost, AIIMS was the Holy Grail for medical students. By 1980, the year Ruit began, it was as competitive to get into as Yale or Harvard in the United States. Every year, more than 75,000 students compete for its 70 positions. Deepak Chopra is one of its most famous graduates. During the first few weeks of Ruit's scholarship, it all seemed too good to be true. 'I walked around the campus pinching myself. *I'd earned a place here?* I was a little incredulous,' he says.

What Ruit probably didn't realise was how much time he would spend with monkeys during his ophthalmology degree in Delhi. As well as seeing 30 or 40 patients a day, and giving tutorial presentations, he wrote a thesis examining whether tuberculosis caused blindness in monkeys. He needed to find out whether the disease swelled the macula, the small area of the retina that humans rely on for reading, writing and seeing colour. About twenty rhesus monkeys were kept in cages on the top floor. As Ruit walked up the last steps and approached the door, he could hear them chattering and leaping about wildly. 'The room looked like a prison, with its iron bars and dim lighting, and smelled like a zoo.'

The keeper was a small, dark, taciturn man who was perpetually chewing betel nuts. There were strict limits to how much time students were allowed in the laboratory, so Ruit took to bribing him so he could stay longer and longer. 'I spent so many hours up there operating on the monkeys that I used money, whisky and fancy cigarettes.'

Together, Ruit and the keeper would catch one of the seven-kilogram packages of muscle, tooth and claw, anaesthetise it, then inject the bacteria into the back of the eyeball to see if it would cause a lesion and an infection, leading to blindness.

With his heart in his mouth, Ruit would open one of the doors with the keeper and after a wrestling match, inject the monkey with Nembutal until it fell asleep. Often it would bite and scratch and Ruit ended up with huge scars all over his arms. Afterwards, the monkeys would be painlessly euthanised.

'Some people might say it's cruel to operate on monkeys, and of course I was appalled at the thought of hurting any living creature. But in those days, it was the only way a cure could be found for diseases such as TB, smallpox and the measles. There are many instances in which great advances have been made in medicine by experimenting on animals.'

It was thanks to his 'long meditations on monkeys' that he was able to master microsurgery, a craft that was in its infancy at that time.

Although AIIMS had the latest microscopes, microsurgery was still a highly specialised skill that took thousands of hours to learn, much like playing the piano or learning ballet. But once Sanduk learnt how to do it, it was like entering a beautiful microscopic universe. Australian ophthalmologist Dr David Moran regards it as 'like going down the rabbit hole in *Alice in Wonderland*, it's like a parallel universe. You learn to step away from yourself. After a while, the process hasn't got much to do with you. You are simply the eyes, the hands and the brains that are going to benefit the patient lying in front of you.'

At first, the subtlest of movements seemed wildly exaggerated under the lens of the microscope. But with endless repetition, straining over the monkey's eyes, about the size of a child's thumbnail, Ruit learnt how to coordinate what he thought he was doing with his hands, and what it looked like through a microscope.

No-one else would go up to the research laboratory. Ruit had the top floor domain all to himself. He would practise all day until his eyes were blurry. Today, when he goes to the monkey temple, Swayambhunath, in Kathmandu and sees the monkeys scampering around, he gives thanks to them. 'It is purely because of the hundreds of hours I spent experimenting on their eyes that I became so skilled in microsurgery. All those hours with them went on to benefit thousands of patients. So, I always tell them how grateful I am.'

It was while Ruit was in New Delhi that eye doctors in the West began using a revolutionary new technique to cure cataracts, an operation that had always been one of the most challenging types of surgery. For centuries, the most common technique for extraction, dating back to the Middle Ages, was a crude technique known as 'couching'. This involved using a curved needle to push the clouded lens into the rear of the eye and out of the patient's field of vision. It was done without an anaesthetic and often resulted in a patient remaining blind or with only partial vision (see Appendix for the history of cataract surgery).

But new advances meant that, if you lived in the West, cataracts had become something that were easily fixed. Days after surgery, patients could return to work, read books, play sport, even sit a driver's test.

'It was completely revolutionary because it finally did away with the thick Coke-bottle glasses,' Ruit says. 'Once any surgeon gets the hang of intraocular lens surgery, it seems like malpractice to do anything else. We knew it was being done on a lot of patients in the West, and that it was very expensive, complicated, and took a long time. But still, everyone was thrilled to think that one day having cataract surgery would be a straightforward procedure. It was an exciting time to be in ophthalmology.'

One of the AIIMS professors who left a lifelong impression on Ruit, Professor Madan Mohan, taught him the art of what he called 'cruising the eye'.

'He was a natural surgeon and a very smooth operator. His surgical skills were beautiful. It looked like he'd never made a mistake. Every movement he made on the surgeon's table had a purpose. The eye is the finest, most delicate tissue in the body, and you need to be extremely careful.' Ruit soaked it all up, watching and then trying to emulate his rhythm, his precision, and the infinite gentleness of his every movement.

'He helped me to fall in love with the eye, which, when you look at it, is an object of great beauty. Every layer, every part of it has been developed by nature and by evolution to perfection. And it's so beautiful to look at, with multiple facets, each perfect, much like a jewel.' He also taught Ruit the art of really caring for his patients. 'He used to say, "Ruit, there's no harm in calling a patient 'Sir' and putting your hand on their shoulder. Nor is there in looking at your patient directly, and explaining quietly and clearly what you are going to do. It doesn't take much to make them feel more comfortable."'" Those teachings in patient care—and the trust and faith that engendered in his patients—were to remain a bedrock in Ruit's career.

Ruit's graduation from medical school in Lucknow had been low-key, but the results of the end-of-year examinations of his postgraduate degree in Delhi saw Ruit basking in the limelight, whether he liked it or not. He had come second in the entire university. It was quite a win for a boy from the border of Tibet, who had grown up expecting to be a salt trader. His peers celebrated by trooping into his dormitory room and pouring rum all over him. Armed with his ophthalmology degree, and doused in spirits, Ruit was finally on his way.

6

EVERY LITTLE THING SHE DOES

Ruit was a newly minted ophthalmologist, in his early thirties, working in the Nepal Eye Hospital, Kathmandu, when he met her. By the mid-1980s, he had started to hit his stride as a surgeon. The speed and dexterity of his work meant Ruit was rapidly earning a reputation as one of the best eye doctors in Nepal.

He was also teaching anatomy to the new ophthalmic assistants, the paramedics who are the lynchpin of the operating theatres, at the Nepal Eye Hospital in the evenings. Tuesday evening became the highlight of his week because a very attractive young woman would always be there, sitting at the end of the second bench, chatting with her friends. Ruit didn't know her name, or anything about her really, other than he liked the way she held herself; she was tall, and had a beautiful posture and a lovely smile. Every day she wore a different coloured sari, or arranged her hair in a different fashion. He was captivated.

He was too shy to talk to her. But he was desperate to impress. The only way he figured he could do that was to make meticulous diagrams of the inner workings of the eye for the lectures. Looking back, he says he can't imagine many women falling in love because they were dazzled by his perfect sketches of the retina or the cornea. At the time, though, it was the only thing he had to offer her.

He would stroll up and down the aisle, making a point of approaching her so that he could see her face, hoping for a sign. Just a flicker of interest. Anything. Sometimes there was just the barest hint of a smile. It was enough to keep the young doctor's hopes alive.

He found out her name was Nanda. When she started assisting in Ruit's operating theatre, he realised she was a first-rate nurse, finely attuned to each of the surgeons, to the point of almost being able to anticipate their needs. And she had those qualities some women have which cannot be taught—she had charm and poise. 'I was filled with a sense of wellbeing just watching her work, and being around her,' he recalls.

But when Ruit asked about her among his friends, his heart sank. She was a Newari woman. Her family was from the prestigious Hindu caste who were the original settlers in Kathmandu, building many of its magnificent ornate palaces and temples.

Ruit, on the other hand, was a Walunga, one of the lowest castes; they comprised the northerners and nomad traders who had migrated to Nepal from Tibet. Nepal's caste system, one of the oldest in the world, segregates people into rigid social tiers according to profession and religion. In those days, it was completely unthinkable for a Newari woman to marry someone of such humble origins.

'It was a completely impossible relationship. I knew we would have been shunned by both our families and that it would be very awkward for everyone,' says Ruit. 'There was so much disapproval of marriages between castes.'

But love was not going to obey the rules. 'When you're really in love, you adore everything about your darling, don't you? I loved the way she walked. Her hairstyles. The way she moved her hands. The way she spoke. She was so pretty, and modest, and had such a lovely attitude, as well as being so caring and practical. I really thought she was the right person for me.'

Ruit had achieved the unthinkable before. He was a village boy who had won a scholarship to study medicine at one of India's most prestigious colleges, and then graduated in ophthalmology at a world-class university in New Delhi. In Nepal, something like this had previously seemed impossible. Could he dare to be as courageous with a relationship as well? To go for what he really wanted, no matter what anyone else said?

'I'm a bit of an introvert but I have a lot of courage. And I have a strong belief in destiny,' Ruit says. A few weeks later, it did seem like the gods were approving of his infatuation. They were both sent to a surgical camp a few hours out of Kathmandu, in the foothills of the Himalaya. 'There was a strong inner voice, telling me that we were meant to be together.' Away from the constraints of Kathmandu, and the scrutiny of society, they could finally talk freely, and at length. Once Ruit could see the attraction was mutual, they went on long walks together. Detached from duty after the day's operations were done, romance blossomed. There were lots of silent glances and meaningful looks. 'No one guessed at all that we were falling in love. We were very careful,' says Ruit. But it was a different matter when they returned to

Kathmandu. The shutters came down. Ruit had to ask Nanda out for about a year before she finally agreed to have tea with him after work.

'She wouldn't say yes, but she didn't say no,' he says. 'She would say "Um, ah, I'm busy", you know, all the things girls can say, or "I have to see my parents". But she kept turning up in the operating theatre, so I knew my interest was not unwelcome. Otherwise, she would have asked to be transferred somewhere else.' It was tantalising to have her working so close by, and yet be so unobtainable.

For almost two years, all he saw of her was her hands, and what he could see of her face above her surgical mask as she buckled down to work in his operating theatre. 'Every now and again, I would ask her out,' he recalls. 'Almost satirically, I would say, "I know you're going to say 'no'," before I asked her out. But, somehow, I knew. I felt there was a strong response inside her even though she didn't express it in words, so I just didn't give up. Our relationship was not a modern type of whirlwind romance. It was much more of a slow-moving river.'

Finally, one day, Nanda agreed to let him take her out to lunch. Ruit was nervous about sharing his dream with her of giving sight to the poorest of people. He was worried she might have been more interested in a comfortable lifestyle rather than something more challenging, but she seemed to approve of the idea.

Their courtship started sedately, with a date once a month, and did not run smoothly. 'When I could see she was falling in love with me a little bit, I told her how much I admired her and that I thought it would be a good idea if we got married. But when she could see how serious I was, she started putting up walls, saying that it was not going to work. I think she brought up the subject at home, and they had been disapproving of the match.'

'There will be so many objections,' she kept telling Ruit. 'I'm Newari, you are Walunga. We simply will not be accepted.' The stakes were high. Nanda was very close to her family, and she was scared of the repercussions, of being ostracised by her family, or worse, completely disowned.

The pair really did look like they came from two different worlds. Nanda was tall, slim and fine boned, so elegant that she could have easily been mistaken for a movie star. Ruit, on the other hand, was a bear of a man; thick set, with broad shoulders, big lungs and strong legs—built, like his ancestors, for durability. Ruit's parents objected to the marriage as well. They kept trying to arrange a match for their son, whose medical degree made him eligible for respectable women from Kalimpong and Darjeeling in India, rather than those from small Nepalese villages. They showed him photographs of attractive young women from good families, encouraging him to meet them.

But it was no use. He had to marry Nanda. He knew instinctively how rare it is to look forward so intensely to meeting up with someone, even for a cup of tea after work. He just didn't give up. 'I'm used to the difficult path, you know,' Ruit says. 'I always expect challenges, and I always knew it was going to be tough for us. She would say, "This is going to be impossible," and I remember saying back to her, "Nothing is impossible." I think you can truly win a woman if you just keep pursuing her, as long as she is interested in you, of course, and your attention is not unwanted.'

Nanda made Ruit work so hard to win her, though, that one day he completely snapped. They were quarrelling in the operating theatre; Nanda was raising her objections to the match, yet again, and in his frustration, Ruit picked up a piece of broken glass and held it over his wrist. "'If you don't marry me!" I said to her, "I'm going to kill myself!"' Then he cut deep into his wrist, several times, drawing blood which spurted all over the floor.

Nanda, horrified, rushed about desperately finding bandages to staunch the flow. Ruit was close to breaking point. 'I was really desperate and it was a kind of threat. It was a bit like, "Today I'm going to cut my wrist, tomorrow you may not see me." And it was true. I really felt like I was going to die if I couldn't be with her.'

His approach worked. They arranged to meet a few days later to work out a plan, and then, finally, Nanda was just looking at him. Not moving her gaze from his face. There was no need for either of them to speak. 'I was so overjoyed I swept her into my arms. I think she knew from that moment on that everything was going to be all right.'

'You know we can't get married here,' she said, 'Our parents will kill us.'

Ruit had been waiting so long to be with her, so he struck while the iron was hot. He'd previously been offered a position in the ophthalmology department at the Academic Medical Center, a large university hospital in Amsterdam, which at the time, had become a world leader in eye surgery. Nanda quickly arranged to work there, too, in the corneal surgery department. They were going to elope to the Netherlands.

They held a simple ceremony in Ruit's apartment on 26 January 1987. They exchanged rings and vows in front of eight friends, then all crammed into his friend Shushil Panta's Volkswagon Beetle and celebrated over lunch at the Shangri-La Hotel. At the time, Ruit had about 7000 rupees or about $50 to his name. The wedding cost half of that. Ruit wore a suit and Nanda wore a maroon sari with a white cardigan. Her hair was swept up off her face in a chignon, showing off pretty earrings.

They flew out of Kathmandu the next week, and were installed in a small rented apartment in Haarlem, a gabled town not far from Amsterdam, surrounded by tulip farms. Ruit was 33, and Nanda was 25. They hardly had any money at all between them, but at long last, they were together. They strolled through the cobblestone streets, and over the canals and bridges, and visited the cathedrals and museums.

It was bitterly cold, and as well as the thrill of finally being together, the young couple both suffered from culture shock. Their senses were overwhelmed by the machinery of Western life. Trams. Lifts. Washing machines. The electronic key of their apartment on the 23rd floor. 'Everything was strange to us. Living in a high rise, electronic doors, and the way people rushed about all the time. We were used to hot *dal* and rice for lunch, and instead we learnt to go to the shops and buy cold sandwiches and apples or peaches,' Ruit says.

One of Ruit's ophthalmologist friends, Jan Kok, took the couple under his wing, taking them out to lunch or dinner almost every day, and quietly explained the cultural subtleties. Those months in Amsterdam were the happiest in their lives. Their work at the hospital was completely absorbing.

Dutch eye doctors such as Jan Worst and Cornelius D Bink-
horst were making great strides in revolutionary cataract
surgery. Up-and-coming surgeons were flying in from
around the globe to make unofficial pilgrimages to see their
work. Ruit revelled in the sophisticated equipment, and
took notes on the finely-honed way the Dutch examined
their patients.

As the time drew nearer for them to return to Kathmandu, Nanda and Ruit grew anxious. There had been no
contact at all with their families; no letters or phone calls
home because they knew their families would be furious with
them when they found out they had eloped. Nanda knew her
brothers had contacted the embassies in both Nepal and the
Netherlands, trying to find out where they were and whether
they'd got married.

As they strolled along the canals, they tried to work out
the next step. They had to think of a way they could stay
together, away from the judgment of Nepalese society.

~

Ruit's mind turned to Professor Fred Hollows, a brilliant,
unorthodox Australian eye doctor he'd befriended two years
previously, in 1985, when Hollows was on a six-week sabbat-
ical, researching the prevalence of trachoma in Nepal for the
World Health Organization.

As a junior doctor at the Nepal Eye Hospital, Ruit had
been sent to collect the professor from Kathmandu's airport.
Ruit was expecting to meet a typical Western eye doctor who,
like so many others, wanted a taste of Third World work
before a holiday trek in the mountains.

Many Western doctors adopted a patronising air when they flew in, conveying the sense, if subtly, to the Nepalese surgeons, that they were lucky to have someone of such calibre at their hospital. It was expected that the Nepalese surgeons would carry their luggage for them at the airport. Local surgeons would humbly ask the visiting Western doctors to finish their operation for them.

But Hollows smashed right through that mould as soon as he landed at Kathmandu airport. It took Ruit a long time to find the Australian because he expected an officious-looking man in a tie and suit. Eventually, a long-haired bloke in an untucked shirt, with a pipe hanging out of the side of his mouth, wandered up to the luggage carousel and said, 'You must be looking for me, are you, mate?'

The pair hit it off from the start. Fred Hollows had made a name for himself as a champion of Australia's Indigenous population. He was horrified when he discovered that the Aboriginal people in remote areas were living in miserable conditions, plagued, among many other diseases, by trachoma, an agonisingly painful infection in the eye that leads to blindness.

Even though the disease had been stamped out in most Western nations more than a century ago, it remained in epidemic proportions in these outback communities, mainly because of overcrowding and lack of clean water. So, Hollows had set off on a gruelling, two-year crusade, belting across the deserts with a small team, treating the local Aborigines and recording the data. The outraged press conferences he held afterwards, highlighting their plight, shamed the government into action. Hollows' was a logistical feat that has not since been repeated and it blazed the trail for making Aboriginal health a priority. Australians loved him for it, and he was later awarded the nation's highest order, the Order of Australia.

Yet, here he was, with no airs or graces whatsoever. Hollows swung his backpack over his own shoulder, reached out to shake hands with Ruit and walked along beside him as if they were equals.

Hollows watched Ruit hard at work at the Nepal Eye Hospital, admiring his extraordinary speed and precision, and began wondering how he could support the brilliant young surgeon. Hollows was eager to join him on the hospital's outreach camps to get a feel for the scope of blindness in rural Nepal. They travelled to remote villages in a jeep, with Ruit at the wheel, and Hollows quickly became as enthralled by the energy and spirit of the cataract camps as Ruit. They dossed down at night in cow sheds, shepherd's huts or tents. Hollows had no problem with instant noodles for dinner as long as it was washed down with gallons of rum and whisky. Ruit recalls that they had to keep sending for alcohol supplies when Hollows came to the camps.

It was at one of these remote camps, near Mount Everest, that the two bonded, and became, as Fred puts it, 'soul mates'. A dwarf had come into the clinic, blind in both eyes from severe cataracts. In Nepal's caste system, a dwarf was untouchable, which means technically he was also untreatable. But Hollows was used to defying convention. He immediately said he'd like to try removing the man's cataracts in the hospital in Kathmandu. Ruit was at first shocked. Then delighted. He gave the man 60 rupees for the bus fare to

Kathmandu and then said: 'Let's stuff it up the noses of those bloody Brahmins [the highest caste, often the doctors] in the eye hospital.'

'I felt like I'd found a brother in ophthalmology,' Ruit says. 'We seemed to understand each other so well. Fred used to hold up his hand and say, "Why are these five fingers so different [in] length, Sanduk? And why are some countries so poor?" I loved every word of our conversations.' Hollows was as brash and outspoken as Ruit was polite and reserved, but they were both obsessively driven about high-quality eye care being the birthright of everyone.

Hollows was as appalled as Ruit by the prevalence of old-style surgeries still being performed in the Nepal Eye Hospital, when, at the same time in the West, intraocular lens transplantation—light years ahead when it came to restoring vision—had become mainstream practice.

Hollows was so smitten by Nepal and his young colleague's vision, he asked his wife Gabi, an orthoptist, to come from Australia to Nepal with their two young children. So, with four-year-old Cam and 27-month-old Emma, whom Gabi was still breastfeeding, the group travelled through the country-side, visiting Ruit's parents in Hille, as well as eye camps.

'Gabi was extremely supportive of my dreams right from the start, sometimes even more so than Fred,' Ruit recalls. 'She was fascinated by it all, and knew the technical details of what we were talking about, which was wonderful.'

Fred and Gabi were deeply impressed by how driven Ruit was and how organised the Nepalese were. They'd done all the research; counting and measuring how many people needed help. It was obvious that Ruit was determined to work out a way to reach the blind. In Gabi's words, 'It was more a matter of working out a way that we could help him.'

Ruit idolised Fred Hollows, not just because he was from the West. He admired the way he treated everyone the same way, whether 'they were a peasant or a king'.

He also admired him because he had no fear. Ruit was trained to be courteous, even when angered. But Hollows just didn't seem to care what anyone thought about him. He would tell government officials, ministers, anyone who was annoying him, to 'Just bugger off'.

During their six weeks together, Hollows had invited Ruit several times to come and visit him in Sydney and learn the latest tricks in the rapidly changing field of cataract surgery. He wanted to show him how things were done at the Prince of Wales Hospital near his home in Randwick, Sydney, where he ran the ophthalmology department.

Now, looking for a safe haven where he and Nanda could begin their married life, he decided to take up Hollows' offer. Ruit rang him from a payphone at the end of the street in Amsterdam. Before the era of Skype and Facetime, such calls were expensive, so he got straight to the point. He suggested it might be the right time to come and visit. He also told Hollows rather sheepishly that he was married.

'His response was just so typically laid-back,' Ruit recalls. 'After a bit of a pause, he just said, "All right, Sanduk! I'd better book two bloody tickets for you then!"'

For the young couple, the offer seemed like manna from heaven. They knew they would face the disapproval of their families once they returned to Nepal, because they had eloped and were of different castes. Within a few days, they had arranged for Australian visas in The Hague and waited for Hollows to send tickets. Instead of flying eastwards back home to Kathmandu, they were going to veer south over the Middle East and boom out over the Indian Ocean, then down to the Great Southern Land.

7

TRAVELLING LIGHT

Ruit was fascinated by his first views out of the plane window as they banked over the Pacific Ocean and flew up the glittering coastline toward Sydney. There just seemed to be so much sea and sky. The blue and green seemed to go on forever. Gabi met them at the airport and drove them back to Farnham House, the rambling sandstone mansion in the leafy eastern suburbs that the Hollows family called home.

It was late summer in Sydney, and the air was heady with the scent of jasmine. The light was so bright it seemed to hurt their eyes. Gabi, as usual, chattered on, hardly pausing for breath. She and Nanda quickly became friends. 'They suited each other perfectly because Gabi talked, and Nanda listened. Gabi always said Nanda made her feel calm,' says Ruit.

The young couple did not know what to make of things when they first arrived at Farnham House. Hollows had bought the 19th-century former convent in the 1970s, and had renovated the dilapidated, eleven-bedroom, tin-roofed building into a home of great warmth and charm. He and Gabi decided they wanted a house that was open to the world as well as a family home, and it quickly came to host an ebb and flow of visitors and long-term house guests. There were seven doors to Farnham House and they were always open to the ocean breeze and a constant stream of visitors. Poets, writers, mountain climbers, Eritrean and Vietnamese surgeons, politicians and filmmakers, as well as Fred and Gabi's seemingly endless extended network of family and friends, all made their way through the doors, day and night.

'Nanda and I thought it was like living at New Delhi railway station,' recalls Ruit. 'After waiting for someone to make us a cup of tea for about three days, we realised it was the fashion to do it yourself.'

They eventually got the hang of it, dangling a tea bag in a mug and getting bread out of the freezer to make their own sandwiches or toast.

Nanda couldn't believe the way there were always empty cups of tea all over the kitchen table, or the kaleidoscope of people who swirled through the dining room and kitchen. One time there were two parties going on simultaneously— one in the back garden, and the other on the front lawn, overlooking the ocean.

But what Farnham House lacked in conventionality was more than compensated for by the way the honeymooners were made to feel welcome. Nanda and Gabi would sit around the open fireplace at night, knitting baby clothes with the other house guests. Fred used to call it the 'Knitting Circle'.

Fred and Gabi's children Cam and Emma would zoom about the verandas on their tricycles while Gabi was nursing their newborn, Anna-Louise, who became Ruit and Nanda's goddaughter. The Hollows family would set a place at the table every night for a 'mystery guest'—anyone they knew who wanted to stay for a while and enjoy the meal and some conversation. It was always filled.

Ruit went to the Prince of Wales Hospital, fifteen minutes' walk up the hill from Farnham House, and practised intra-ocular lens surgery every day with state-of-the-art equipment. Hollows looked over Ruit's shoulder as he effortlessly sur-passed him in technical skill and speed. It was obvious to Fred and Gabi that Ruit was remarkably talented. They had a star in the making. They called him 'Golden Hands'.

Nanda melted into family life with the Hollows. She would walk up to the Prince of Wales Hospital and join Ruit for lunch several times a week. She helped Gabi take Cam to school. She'd hold Emma's hand while Gabi pushed Anna-Louise in her pram through the parks or down the hill toward Coogee Bay, trying to cajole her baby to sleep.

Gabi correctly assumed that the young couple didn't have much money. 'We didn't tell her, but we actually had almost nothing at all,' Ruit says. 'She knew we were too shy to ask, so she would just quietly tuck money into our pockets.'

They went to nearby Bronte Beach, sat on the grass over-looking the ocean, enjoyed barbecues in the park, dreamed, and talked about the future. They went bushwalking in the Blue Mountains to the west of Sydney, and were embraced by the fifteen or so other Nepalese living in Sydney at the time, such as Indra Ban, who later formed the Nepalese Australian Association.

The Nepalese would gather in each other's homes, speak their mother tongue and cook Nepalese food. Ban's heart went out to Nanda, who was 'so shy she hardly said anything. It must have been a huge shock for her to be in such a different culture.'

'It was a wonderful year for Nanda and me to get to know each other without the pressure of society around us. It also gave me a year to think about the big picture, and what I wanted to achieve when we got back home,' Ruit says. 'We had such a beautiful year in Sydney.'

Fred and Ruit would sit up late into the night, outside on the veranda in the summer, drinking too much whisky and scotch as they talked about how to wipe out avoidable blindness.

They were united in their outrage that the governments of developing countries were unwilling or unable to spend the money to look after the poorest people. Ruit's bold vision earned Gabi's admiration.

'It was obvious, right at the start, that he was going to move mountains if he had to, to see it through. Fred would have been so proud of him, because he's just kept plugging away doggedly at the task. Fred said shortly before he died, "You know, if all I've achieved is launching Ruit, then my life's been a success, because I know he'll change the world."'

Despite Fred's colourful language and crotchety moods, there was undoubtedly a real connection between the two of them.

Ruit was looking for leadership from the Western world and he certainly found it in Hollows. He was enthralled by his friend's first-rate mind and conversation.

Hollows used to love the storms that rolled in over nearby Coogee Bay, several kilometres south of Bondi Beach. Hollows would stand on the sandstone veranda, gazing out at the lightning over the bay and shout to the heavens, 'Come on, send her down, will you! Send the rain down!'

The Australian journalist Ray Martin often joined Hollows and Ruit at Farnham House and was struck by the deep accord between the pair and the way they were both hypnotised by the thrill of helping people see.

'Fred was always such a cock-eyed optimist. I knew that, in the real world, the money just wasn't there, so I thought to myself, *Dream on* . . . The two of them were like soul brothers.' But they were both mesmerised, intoxicated by the power of giving people the gift of sight. Fred would say, 'This is too f--king good. This is the sort of medicine you don't need to get paid to do!'

Ruit was of the same opinion, even though he didn't use the same language. It could be seen in Ruit's face, the same deep satisfaction as he unwrapped the bandages, shining a light in the eyes of a patient and witnessing them seeing the world.

Martin interviewed Hollows and Ruit on *The Midday Show*, a popular television show that ran for decades in Australia. They passed a hat around the audience—mainly middle-aged housewives—and raised a few hundred dollars for Ruit's work.

'Ruit was incredibly shy to interview,' Martin recalls. 'He really thought that without Fred he would have been a humble eye doctor in the Third World. Fred was the inspiration who launched him up to the next level.'

Ruit and Nanda's year of sunshine and freedom was drawing far too quickly to an end. They were tempted by the idea of staying in Australia, enabling Ruit to take a well-paid position.

But the gravitational pull back home to Kathmandu was strong. Ruit needed to help his own people—'the most deserving people in the world'.

Although Fred and Gabi weren't well-off themselves at this stage, they set up a support group for Ruit at their kitchen table. The Nepal Eye Program Australia or NEPA, as it was called, started with about $2000 to its name. The first donation of $500 came from the Nepalese Australian Association which had raised the money by hiring a hall at the Prince of Wales Hospital, where they showed slides of Ruit's work curing the blind, and served homemade Nepalese dumplings, tea and coffee.

NEPA was small, but it was stacked with talent. The president of 'Ruit's cheer squad', as Dr David Moran refers to it, who gathered around Fred and Gabi's kitchen table, was Tim Macartney-Snape, the first Australian to climb to the summit of Mount Everest.

The tiny support group grew into the biggest success story in Nepal. What made it work was that there was always a great deal of trust involved. Everyone in NEPA believed wholeheartedly in Ruit.

Hollows drove Ruit and Nanda to Sydney airport with duffle bags full of intraocular lenses, the tiny sequin-like pieces of plastic that, at $200 each, are worth their weight in gold in Nepal. Hollows had no hesitation plundering supplies if it was for the disadvantaged.

Setting up the first free Aboriginal Medical Service several years earlier, he had reversed a truck into the storage cupboards of the Prince of Wales' pharmacy and helped himself to as many medical supplies and equipment as he could fit into the back. For his young Nepalese friend, Hollows had no hesitation liberating lenses for a higher calling. He begged, borrowed or procured as many from surgical companies as he could.

Although Nanda had missed her family, the thought of returning home filled her with trepidation. Traditionally, when Nepalese go to the West to work, they bring back household equipment, clothes, toys, and, most importantly, money, to be distributed among family and friends. As Ruit and Nanda had not worked, they had nothing to offer—other than intraocular lenses, and Ruit's audacious dream of wiping out avoidable blindness in his country.

They knew it was going to be hard when they went back home to face the disapproval of their family, but nothing prepared them for just how shunned they would feel.

No-one was there to meet them at the airport. Not one person. And no-one was prepared to take them into their home. They lived very simply for about a month with one of Ruit's friends, in a run-down flat with a shared bathroom outside. They had only a few rupees between them and kept to a simple diet of porridge, and rice and curry. Nanda had led a very sheltered life, protected by her family. Now, because of her marriage, she was living in a small flat on her own all day, isolated from her relatives, and almost completely broke. 'It was a really tough time for Nanda. I felt terrible,' Ruit says. The only consolation he could think of was to constantly reassure her with the phrase: 'I am your father, your mother, your brother, your husband.' He made sure she felt comfortable all the time, and that she had his total support.

Nanda's brothers and sisters finally paid a visit, six months after the couple had returned home. They told Nanda that she could come back home whenever she wanted to, which was a polite, Nepalese way of saying that they didn't approve of the match at all. But Nanda had no regrets. She was in love with her husband, and focused on building a life with him.

Ruit's father was the first to give his tacit consent to the marriage by allowing the couple to live in a small flat that he owned, above a photo shop, and under his own apartment, on a busy road near the Bagmati River, not far from the Nepal Eye Hospital. The days were long for Nanda. She was on her own, with not a soul to talk to, from 7.45 a.m. when Ruit left for work until often 8 p.m. when he returned home. Sonam, being a thrifty trader, was dividing his time between his flat in the capital city and Hille where Kasang and the rest of his family continued to live. Despite the fact that Nanda cooked for Sonam whenever he was in Kathmandu, such was the rigidity of the caste system in Nepal at the time, that he completely ignored her. He refused to talk to her.

Not only had his son married a Hindu, but he had married someone from a different caste.

Ruit regards their time as outcasts as one that bolstered their marriage. 'I think being shunned by our families drew us closer together. It made us put extra effort into our relationship. The obstacles we faced only seemed to make us grow closer. It made us really strong, because there was no one else around to lean on. We had to rely on each other.'

And besides, Ruit knew there was one sure way he could cut right through the prejudice and restore their place in society: by becoming one of the country's finest doctors.

8

AGAINST THE WIND

By 1988, when Ruit had returned to the Nepal Eye Hospital, he had refined intraocular cataract surgery to the point where the wound was so tiny that no stitches were needed at all and his patients' eyes healed of their own accord.

The self-healing surgery was far less expensive and much safer than the older style of surgery. No glasses were fitted afterwards. At the first outreach camps he organised, funded by the hospital and the World Health Organization, he witnessed how truly life-transforming the self-healing surgery was for patients. They could literally get up and walk home on their own with perfect vision a few days after surgery.

Ruit wasn't the only one working on the revolutionary technique, but no-one else was prepared to take on such a colossal task as travelling on foot, or horseback, or a rattling old bus, for days on end, to take the new technique to some of the most remote communities on earth.

He was on the threshold of developing a system of modern cataract surgery that could transform eye care in Nepal, and right through the developing world. The time was ripe to get started.

Yet, in what would become one of the most monumental frustrations of Ruit's life, the senior eye doctors showed no interest in adopting the new techniques. He met a brick wall of opposition every time he raised the subject. The harsh reality began to dawn that he might have to leave the security of his position at the Nepal Eye Hospital and strike out on his own to achieve his lofty ambition.

Ruit was so low, he was at the point of despair.

Working on the national survey into blindness, he had seen first-hand the devastating numbers of Nepalese who were left blind, simply because they were unable to make it to a clinic or hospital and receive modern eye care. He was desperate to start changing things for the better. He longed for intraocular lenses and portable microscopes, to start setting up clinics in rural areas. But every time he tried to make a start, Nepali bureaucracy came down on him like a tonne of bricks. As a junior doctor at a government hospital, he had no authority or clout. His suggestions were met with snide remarks. He knew that to turn his vision into reality, he needed to break away from the government hospital, and the inertia and corruption that accompanied it. But it was a daunting task. The stakes were high. To do so would be seen as treason by the ophthalmic hierarchy.

The big stumbling block was that each intraocular lens cost about $200, which would take a Nepalese villager about six months to earn. Although the Nepalese elite could fly to Delhi or Bangkok, Thailand, for a state-of-the-art operation, the price tag of those little pieces of plastic kept them well out of reach of the estimated 600,000 blind in Nepal.

As well as being expensive, they were hard to obtain. Ruit's only source were outdated versions from the West. The rapidly changing designs in intraocular lenses meant that manufacturers were able to donate the older ones that still worked well to the developing world. His work had begun attracting the attention of surgeons from the West, who were fascinated by his cause and wanted to help. Every time American doctors such as Richard 'Dick' Litwin flew into Kathmandu, Ruit would ask them, 'Don't forget to bring me a box of eyes, will you?'

Litwin, a laid-back Californian, became known as 'Santa Claus', not just for his snowy white beard, but because he never failed to turn up at Kathmandu airport without duffle bags filled with the feather-light lenses. He would charm his way through customs by telling the officials that they were to 'help your grandmothers see again'. Litwin's sweet-talking worked every time, but Ruit knew it was not a long-term solution to solving the heartbreaking backlog of patients needing cataract surgery.

The more Ruit tried to persuade his superiors to adopt modern cataract surgery, the more they declined to engage in his idea. Some of his adversaries were openly hostile. 'Stop dreaming, Sanduk. You don't have the equipment—or the lenses—to do it,' they would tell him; 'It's never going to happen. What you're trying to suggest is impossible. It's just far too expensive.'

They argued the case, telling him that for every $200 spent on one intraocular lens, 50 older-style surgeries with glasses could be performed. They pointed out that there were not enough trained surgeons who knew how to do modern cataract surgery. 'They're very complicated to insert,' his opponents would argue. 'That's fine for you to go out there and operate on someone's eye, but who is going to go back and do the second one?'

They threw every trick in the book at him. The one that truly galled him was the accusation that the technique had not been proven by clinical trial.

'But it has been proved in the West,' Ruit would reply wearily. 'They've shown it works on white people, they just haven't done trials to show it works in the developing world as well.' He knew prejudice was at play, and there was nothing he could do about it.

He was hamstrung. In retrospect, Ruit says, carrying out a clinical trial would have probably helped his approach to become accepted much faster, but at the time, it was an impossible task. The Nepal Eye Hospital was on a shoestring budget and an enormous amount of time and money was needed to conduct a clinical trial. Large numbers and clear protocols were required to analyse it properly.

'Everyone in the ophthalmology field knew that intra-ocular surgery would work extremely well in the developing world. All you really need is a clean room, sterile equipment and a good team.'

Ruit remained impeccably polite in the face of disapproval, but what his critics didn't realise was that he'd become completely enthralled with the new technique. There was no turning back for him. Every time he did an intraocular lens operation, he was quietly musing about how he could train a squadron of doctors to perform them throughout the developing world; how to reduce the prices of the lenses; how to obtain robust, portable microscopes that could be bundled up onto buses, jeeps, and onto the backs of horses to be taken to far-flung valleys and up to remote mountain tops. He was obsessively driven about applying his technique to the worst pockets of blindness in Nepal.

He grew enraged that a second-rate treatment was being tolerated, even championed by his peers. All he could see was that hundreds of thousands of people were getting second-class treatment, or remaining blind, simply because the Nepal Eye Hospital was threatened by the new technique. He met patients fitted out with glasses who had slipped so many times on the terraces in the monsoon season that they were covered in bruises and scratches. Many patients lost or broke their glasses and were unable to replace them; there are very few spectacle shops in the Himalayas.

'It was really hard for Ruit,' recalls Litwin. 'He wasn't in charge of the hospital, but his heart was with the Nepalese people and he could see the government wasn't going to help. He must have felt so held back. The intraocular lenses weren't just a threat in the Nepal Eye Hospital, they were a threat to an entire generation of ophthalmic surgeons in the US as well. It meant they would have to learn a whole new way of cataract surgery and many retired rather than convert to the new procedure. A lot of older ophthalmologists resisted and disapproved of the new technique.'

Ruit's main opponent for many years was the head of the Nepal Eye Hospital, Dr Ram Prasad Pokhrel. 'RP', as he was known, didn't like his brilliant young protégé breaking away from his empire. 'He didn't say "No" up front, but his body language was critical. His body language was that he wouldn't endorse it,' Ruit recalls.

Ruit's homelife meant a great deal to him as he faced such tough opposition. Nanda had grappled with her new role at first as a stay-at-home wife. She was a highly accomplished ophthalmic assistant, widely respected at the hospital, and had initially been reluctant to give up her career. But as Ruit's hours grew longer and longer, and the scope of his vision grew clearer, they settled on traditional marriage, with well-defined roles. Ruit was the breadwinner and Nanda did the shopping, organised the cooking, and packed Ruit's bags when he set off on a trip.

'I don't think he's ever held a shopping bag in his life,' Nanda likes to say. 'We joke it's because it might wreck his hands.'

'I know Nanda has always appreciated how hard I work,' says Ruit. 'I worked such long hours at the hospital and she never complained. She's never intruded on my work or tried to interfere. She just never doubted that everything would work out. Having her by my side has been the greatest gift.'

Ruit's devotion to Buddhist teachings was also a mainstay. His commitment to several Buddhist teachers—and awe of some of them—stems from his father's own unswerving devotion. The memory of Sonam, sitting crossed-legged at his shrine before dawn every morning in their wooden house in Walung, saying prayers to the deity Guru Rinpoche, was stamped in his psyche. 'I saw my father as the epitome of moral values. I knew instinctively that his moral compass had been shaped by Buddhism, so I was naturally drawn to the same teachers as well.'

Although Ruit didn't go to temples, his commitment to the teachings of the Buddha imbued all his actions, and gave him courage and strength in times of adversity.

'In a complex situation or a challenge, if the problems keep coming, then very often I shut my eyes and I get this bright pool of light in front of me. I know it's come from the teachers I've met,' he says. 'All I know is that it gives me a very relaxed feeling of taking on challenges and problems. It's always a relief after I close my eyes and see this bright phenomenon coming. Afterwards, the problem doesn't seem to bother me.'

~

Ruit was forced to draw on his faith as he faced the increasingly loud chorus of complaints against his work. Things came to a head in 1989 when the International Association for the Prevention of Blindness held a conference in Kathmandu. The agenda was 'To discuss the latest developments in intraocular surgery', but it would be safe to assume that its aim was to put the audacious young surgeon firmly back in his place.

Says Ruit: 'We were doing sophisticated surgery in the bush and that was making the big five-star surgeons uneasy. They thought, *What are these bastards doing?* There were a lot of people who were threatened by what we were doing.'

The conference was held at Hotel Yak & Yeti, the finest conference hotel in town, complete with ornate mirrors and soaring ceilings. The foyer was decorated with potted palms and banners to welcome twenty of the best ophthalmologists from around the world. One of them was the legendary Dr Govindappa Venkataswamy, or 'Dr V', from Aravind Hospital in Madurai, India, with whom Ruit had worked during his ophthalmology postgraduate degree. Dr V, who set up Aravind Hospital in the 1970s as a non-profit institution, was a philanthropic surgeon and a guiding light for young surgeons like Ruit. Despite being afflicted by rheumatoid arthritis and finger deformities, he performed thousands of sight-restoring operations. Empowered by his spiritual guru, Sri Aurobindo, he regarded his work more as a sacred task or calling than a job. 'His leadership, spirituality and commitment to his patients were unforgettable,' Ruit says.

Ruit felt sick with nerves as he walked into the conference. He was not a good public speaker but he desperately needed to show his peers his team's superb results implanting intraocular lenses in remote villages.

A group of doctors began showing slides of the old-style surgery for cataracts. Fred Hollows had returned to Nepal for the conference to support Ruit. The two comrades sat next to each other and grew white with rage as they listened.

'Thousands of cases of surgery without intraocular lenses. How could anyone be proud of using these old-school techniques?' Ruit recalls. 'Why would you boast about a technique that left people with inferior vision?'

Ruit's hands were sweating, and his heart was racing. His mind was filled with the herculean efforts his team had gone to in order to provide world-class eye care in the toughest conditions. He thought of the bus rooftops his team had clung on to, the mountains they'd trekked with heavy packs and baskets, packed to the gunnels with medical equipment. He thought of his father, Sonam, who told him, 'Whenever there is an easy road, and a hard one, son, always take the hard one.'

When it was time for Ruit to speak, he walked up to the stage, clutching his notes. His guts were going berserk. A hush fell over the delegates.

Ruit put his head down and stuck to his notes. Stiff and awkward, he doggedly ploughed through his speech, showing slides of the successful intraocular lens implantations they'd done in the countryside. The news was met with a stony silence. Then, as Ruit recalls, 'Everyone just stood up and said, "Shit, you're not allowed to do that!" It was a real uproar. They were outraged. They were raising their hands, and a representative from the World Health Organization asked why we hadn't done a clinical trial.'

The comments of one dapper doctor wounded him to the core. 'This gentleman told me that I should stop talking such nonsense.' Ruit says. 'He said that we simply could not afford to help everyone in the way I wanted to. He said that for every blind person I cured with an intraocular lens for $200, they could cure 60 or 70 with old-style surgery and old-style glasses. He said there were far more important things to be talking about and that I should sit down and stop wasting everybody's time.'

Years of painstaking work had just been snuffed out like a candle. It was as if the entire ophthalmology community was against him. He felt enraged that the validity of his work was being called into question.

Despite his nerves, Ruit would not be silenced.

'Somehow, I found my voice,' he recalls. 'The words were faint at first, but I managed to get out what I wanted to say to the delegates. I asked them, "If your son or daughter was blind, would you want him or her to lie on their bed without moving all week, after their lenses had been taken out, and then fitted with thick glasses which they would probably lose or break? And what about all the people who can't even get to a hospital? The ones who can't afford the bus fare, or who can't read or write, and don't even know that help is available and that they can get their eyes fixed? We need to think about them as well. We have a duty to look after them as well. And if they can't get to us, we need to go to them!"'

Hollows was renowned for his explosive candour, and, just in case Ruit wasn't forthright enough, he walked up onto the stage, and told them what *he* thought of their attitude.

'I can't repeat what Fred said because of the colourful language, but it was along the lines of: "One day, you mark my words, the World Health Organization will recommend intraocular lenses, just like Ruit is doing, rather than those ridiculous Coke-bottle glasses. And you bloody American imperialists will be eating humble pie."'

Then Hollows turned to the other delegates in the room, glared at them over his glasses, and abused them for clinging to a second-rate method. 'He told them they were bloody fools, that they were colonial upstarts, sitting there on their arses knowing they were giving world-class eye care to rich white people, and second-rate care to the people in their own backyard. He told them they should be ashamed of themselves. You could hear people gasping. Their mouths literally dropped open.'

British-born ambulance driver Rex Shore, who acted as Ruit's scribe, translator, secretary, engineer, postman and driver, was waiting anxiously in the foyer. The pair had met in Sydney, where Ruit had asked him to 'help with a dream he had'. Shore, already infatuated with Nepal, resigned from his job, booked a flight to Kathmandu, and quickly proved invaluable, drafting endless letters for Ruit and becoming a jack-of-all-trades.

'Ruit came out looking terribly flustered and saying to Fred, "I wish you wouldn't speak like that!"' Shore recalls.

Ruit and Hollows salved their battle wounds at the hotel bar. After a couple of strong whiskies, Ruit realised that he could never go back to the establishment. He was regarded as an outlaw. A renegade. A madman, even. And it was strangely liberating.

Ruit's dogged refusal to back down and fall into line, his inability to accept mediocrity and play by the rules, meant many of his colleagues began to have a grudging respect for him. Many people in the ophthalmic world began to be swept into 'the cause'. They wanted to be part of Ruit's wild utopian dream.

9

MAVERICKS

The year after Ruit and Nanda had moved back to Kathmandu from Sydney, they were kept firmly at arm's length
by his family. The ostracism continued, even if they'd been
invited to lunch at Ruit and Nanda's flat, and Nanda had
cooked an elaborate meal. His family would talk among
themselves, completely ignoring her, despite her hospitality.

Nanda put her head down, kept cooking, and remained
quietly confident that one day they would accept the marriage.
Her instincts were right. One day, her in-laws finally looked at
her as she was serving them lunch. It was one of the happiest
days of her early married life with Ruit.

The rift was finally healed with the arrival of Sagar,
their first child, in 1989, almost exactly a year after they
had returned to Nepal. Sagar was a healthy, bright-eyed
3.9-kilogram boy, and Sonam and Kasang were yearning to
see and hold their own flesh and blood.

The couple took Sagar to Hille when he was about eight
months old. That led to a full reconciliation. It was really

then that their unofficial marriage was accepted. Kasang gave Nanda her traditional wedding dress to wear and the couple exchanged rings again, this time with their whole family as witnesses. 'It was very touching, we felt really accepted,' Nanda recalls. Kasang and Sonam began visiting Nanda and Sagar in Kathmandu, keen to spend time with their plump little grandson.

'I'll never forget the moment when I had a sudden glimpse of family togetherness. It was wonderful. It meant so much to us,' Ruit recalls.

Sagar's first birthday, in 1990, marked another major milestone in Ruit's life. That was the year he decided to walk out of the gates of the Nepal Eye Hospital for the last time. He was heading into the field to do modern cataract surgery himself, and to eventually set up his own hospital, even if it meant being a scourge to the establishment. Perhaps something of his mentor's attitude had finally rubbed off on him. 'Don't tell me what you can't bloody do,' Hollows would say. 'Tell me how you're going to do it.'

Ruit's departure sent shockwaves through the ophthalmic community. Ram Pokhrel was furious when he heard the news that Ruit was resigning, and that NEPA, the Australian charity supporting him, was withdrawing its funding.

Pokhrel was Brahmin, the highest caste. He was used to having total control over the hospital and he didn't want to lose the talented young doctor.

But once Ruit took a deep breath, and stepped out of the system, nothing could shake his resolution.

Even with such a strong inner guidance to rely on, Ruit could not do this kind of work on his own. He needed a loyal team to help shoulder the load. He has an uncanny flair for choosing the right people for the job. He watches them carefully, gets the measure of them, before he asks for their help. It's rare that his instincts are wrong.

Ruit chose seven staff, whom he later dubbed 'The Magnificent Seven', from the Nepal Eye Hospital to help run his microsurgical camps. All excelled in their work. And all of them, he figured, believed in him enough to take a big risk and to handle the physical hardships involved.

Ruit called them into his tiny office in the small, private practice he'd set up soon after graduating to help support his family. During his six years working at the Nepal Eye Hospital, Ruit's typical day had involved working from 8 a.m. until 4.30 p.m. at the hospital, earning a salary that was about 2500 rupees (AU$30) a month. To supplement his income, he also worked most nights, from 4.30 p.m. to 9 p.m., at his own practice in New Road, charging private patients a small fee to prescribe them glasses. 'My private practice was never for operations. I could have easily done that, and made an enormous amount of money, but neither Nanda nor I felt it was a good example to set.' Now this tiny room was to become the unofficial headquarters for his campaign.

Over cups of extra sweet *chia*, Ruit outlined his plan to take modern eye surgery to every corner of Nepal. 'I don't know if I'll succeed or not, but I have a strong feeling this will work,' he told them.

The Nepal Eye Program (NEP) charity was formed to support Ruit's work, along with NEPA in Australia.

NEP had only $200 to its name, but it had heft. Shambhu

Tamang, the youngest person to ascend Mount Everest, advised on camp logistics, and Hari Bansha Acharya, one of the country's most popular actors, helped with publicity. The legal adviser was Sushil Pant, who later became the country's attorney-general.

Today, working with Ruit is seen as a prestigious position, but, back then, venturing with Ruit to the outreach camps was truly leaping into the unknown.

'I encouraged them to join me by telling them that I'd handpicked them all for their special qualities; a combination of technical skill and good hearts. I told them that although our country wasn't doing anything for the blind, our small group might be able to actually make a difference if we tried.' All of them said yes.

One of them was Nabin Rai, a talkative young assistant, smart, kind and trustworthy—'the sort of person you'd depend upon in a life crisis' as Ruit puts it. Rai had a flair for coordinating with far-flung villages, and is still working with Ruit as the medical coordinator at Tilganga. He also asked two nurses, Beena Sharma and Karuna Shrestha, if they would join his medical caravan. Rex Shore would tease them by calling them 'The Princesses' because they were so pretty, as well as being tonnes of fun. Both are still working by Ruit's side in the operating theatre. Despite their gentle voices, they run a trim ship.

Dr Reeta Gurung, the current CEO of Tilganga, was also tapped on the shoulder. Gurung was cut from the same cloth as Ruit, having grown up in a small rural village with no school. She had the same focus and determination as Ruit and forged a reputation as a brilliant surgeon, with a steady, even temperament that earned her the nickname 'Cool-hand Gurung.'

'I burst into tears when he asked me to join his band of outlaws,' she says. 'There was no doubt in my mind that I was going to work for him, and it was going to lead to great things. Ruit was working on the new technique and we knew it would be a breakthrough. Our aim was simple. To avoid the papers and protocols. To get away from the system and just go out and do it. That's what united us all.'

And of course, there was his ever-faithful right-hand man, Rex Shore.

With the team first assembled, they did the work under-cover. No fanfare. No permission asked. They just did it. Ruit didn't even tell Fred Hollows that he'd started doing the new intraocular lens surgery at the camps. 'Nobody knew about it,' Ruit says. 'I started in a very quiet way. If I'd let people know about it, they would have killed me.'

Meanwhile, Shore would hire any transport he could find to reach the most underprivileged villages. These were usually battered old buses from India with dodgy engines, worn old tyres, with a top speed of about 30 kilometres an hour. They christened one rattling old jeep from Russia 'Khrushchev', and another from China 'Mao'. At one stage, they hired a tractor to drive their surgical equipment up to a village at the top of the mountain.

They'd always start the night before, packing all the equipment they'd need to set up their makeshift surgeries: anaesthetics, syringes, green surgical drapes, face masks, caps, rolls of gauze, scalpels, forceps, sutures and medical tape, and black plastic to line the walls for hygiene. Also, boxes of donated intraocular lenses, and, if they were lucky, some basic microscopes. If the region they were going to had no electricity, they would bundle a generator onto the bus as well.

The jeep or bus was often so cramped that they had to take turns riding on the roof. Anyone unlucky enough to be on the top had to grip the rails as they teetered on the cliff's edge, just inches away from precipitous drops below. Ruit sat on the roof a couple of times, but was usually inside, nursing a precious microscope on his lap.

It was a terrifying way to travel, swinging wildly around hairpin bends with crumbling cliff edges, brightly decorated buses bearing down on them from the opposite direction with their musical horns blaring. Both vehicles would come to a shuddering halt as they negotiated who would go around the bend first. Often there were no road barriers, and the roads were scenes of carnage. Buses and trucks that had plummeted over the edge were a frequent sight.

One tragic night, a bus rolled off a cliff nearby and injured passengers had been brought to a local clinic. Ruit and his team rushed in to find about 30 people lying quietly in a room on tables. 'Many were quiet because they were dead,' recalls Dick Litwin, the Californian doctor whom Ruit had befriended years earlier.

Safety improved when they managed to scrounge enough money to buy an old bus of their own. Shore adapted it by pulling out the back seats for the equipment.

Ruit and his team relied on word of mouth to notify locals about the outreach camps. They would let the local police station, radio station and school know which day they were arriving. The boy scouts would go door-to-door.

Ruit's team would spend the first day setting up a camp, using anything from local clinics, veterinary clinics, school houses and monasteries as operating theatres. Once or twice during the Nepalese Civil War between 1996 and 2006, when a group of rebels known as the Maoists tried to overthrow the Nepalese monarchy, the team even used rebel army posts.

Once they had established an impromptu theatre, they would brush out the cobwebs, sweep out the dung and the straw, tape plastic over the ceiling to prevent any mice or rats in the roof from falling onto the operating table, and tape up the windows with heavy cloth or newspaper. They would swab the place down with antiseptic. If there was nothing else available, kitchen tables or school desks were borrowed, and placed end to end, to use as operating tables.

The recovery rooms were just as rustic. After their operations, the patients were often laid out on crude beds of straw in barns or cowsheds. At night, the team would sleep in tents, barns, haylofts or as guests with local families.

Ruit started off quietly, doing a handful of intraocular lens surgeries at each camp. As his confidence grew, he did more and more, so that eventually almost all the operations used the new technique. 'I went very, very slowly, to make absolutely certain there were no mistakes. The pressure to succeed was intense. It was like living on a knife's edge. I had so many critics in the ophthalmic world that I knew I could not make the tiniest mistake,' he says. He knew that what he was doing—providing high-quality, inexpensive eye surgery in one of the most underprivileged countries in the world— was a grand experiment. If he could do it in Nepal, it could be done anywhere.

The backlog was immense. No one knows why the rate of cataracts is so high in Nepal. It might have to do with diet or altitude, or exposure to sunlight. The lack of access to doctors, clinics and medical help certainly made the problem worse. As did the prevalent belief that cataracts were an inevitable part of ageing.

'There is a saying in many of the villages: first your hair goes white, then your eyes go white, then you die,' Ruit says. 'It's a fatalistic acceptance of blindness that we are still trying to educate a lot of villagers about.'

Ruit rang Hollows after he felt confident with the results he was getting. He remembers the long pause at the end of the line as Hollows digested the news. 'You're doing IOLs out in the bush, Sanduk? Jesus f--cking Christ, what about the f--king infection rates?'

The truth was, the infection rates were extremely low, lower than in the hospitals, in fact, even though he didn't have surgical gloves and they were operating on dirt floors. Ruit's team sterilised every piece of equipment scrupulously, endlessly swabbing them with alcohol or washing them in steam sterilisers that looked like giant pressure cookers. The highest risk of infection after eye surgery is if the wound or cut in the eye from the surgery is not well constructed and ends up leaking. If it seals properly and is completely watertight, as Ruit ensured, then the risk of infection was very low.

Fred and Gabi Hollows were so impressed by Ruit's results in the field that they donated a new Toyota LandCruiser, which Rex named Hilda, after the valiant Nordic Valkyrie. 'She was a good and faithful vehicle,' he says. 'She lived up to her name, battling blindness in the mountains of Nepal.'

At every camp, usually funded by Ruit's support groups in Australia and Nepal, two or three hundred blind people would make their way to the screening tables for help. Shore, a highly methodical man, was horrified to see the more desperate patients pushing and shoving to get in for surgery. 'There were hundreds and hundreds of patients, and it was so chaotic. There was no system about it at all, it was just madness.'

NEPA printed forms for Shore, enabling him to list each patient's name, address, as well as their screening and operation results. Everything else was recorded in exercise books. They worked out a way to explain to the patients what was going to happen to them—an early form of counselling that is a mainstream part of hospitals today. After the operations, they would drum into the patients how important follow-up care was; that they had to take their eye drops, and come back for a check-up a few weeks later.

There was an incredible energy, gusto and pace to the camps. Morale was high. It's easy to understand why someone from the Walunga tribe would love being outdoors, up in the foothills or the mountains, with the wind on his face, and the sun on his back, helping the people who needed his help the most. It's where Ruit felt he belonged. Here, he was not seen as an interloper or a troublemaker. Out here he was mobbed by patients, and sometimes even revered as a god. Nanda says that today, more than three decades later, her husband's idea of a perfect holiday remains 'somewhere picturesque in the mountains where he can do 70 cataract surgeries a day, and for the whole family to come along with him'.

Over the next ten years, Ruit's team travelled to every

corner of Nepal, India, China and Bhutan. They performed the new intraocular surgery on every person who could make it to their microsurgical camps, no matter what caste or tribe, no matter how rich or poor. They operated on the Brahmin, Chetri and Newari people, as well as the Sherpa, Rai, Gurung, Tamang, Limbu, Tharu and Madhesi. They operated on single mothers, children, grandfathers, farmers, teachers—even, during the ten-year civil war, on rebel soldiers. They operated on the downtrodden and the deaf, even the untouchables (the lowest caste in India).

In many remote regions, such as Tibet, Mustang and Bhutan, the locals often came up to touch Ruit on the arm, or they took his hand and placed it on top of their head as a form of blessing. They'd ask him to bless their children, or request a lock of his hair. They'd prostrate before him on the ground, or stick their tongues out reverentially. (The practice of sticking out one's tongue began, as legend has it, because an evil king in Tibet had a black tongue; out of respect, the Tibetans often stick out their tongues to show they are not evil.)

They regarded Ruit as a miracle worker because they felt he had given them their lives back.

There was nothing mystical about the procedure, though. It was a thoroughly modern one. The real miracle was giving them the same advantages as anyone else in the world.

~

The work Ruit had committed himself to was physically exhausting, however. He and his team made house calls that sometimes involved trudging uphill for days with a portable surgery strapped to the back of packhorses.

'I knew my exit from the eye hospital was like walking on a sword's edge. I accepted that challenge. I talked about it with Nanda. For me, it's just how the world works. When something is a struggle, rather than a smooth ride, it makes you very strong. I knew the best way was to just go out and do it, and do everything so well that it proved everyone wrong. When you have people who are critical of you, it makes you do things properly. It's the best kind of challenge. In a way, I was always used to being against the crowd. I knew I had the strength to face the worst.'

What Ruit wasn't prepared for was that the criticism would go on unrelentingly for years, and how it would corrode his health. Not long after he'd started running the microsurgical camps, a group of senior doctors wrote a letter to the prime minister, Girija Prasad Koirala, complaining that Ruit had no right to be doing intraocular lens surgery in the mountain villages without having done a clinical trial. Fortunately, Ruit had been asked to operate on the prime minister's eye shortly after they sent their letter. As Koirala came into Ruit's clinic, he said with an amused look on his face, 'I see your friends have been complaining about you again, Dr Ruit?' Nothing more came of it.

The undermining led to long bouts of insomnia. 'I'd pace around the flat, trying to work out a solution, and a long-term plan,' recalls Ruit. 'I knew there were a lot of people who would criticise and even put me in jail if anything went wrong.'

His blood pressure soared sky-high under so much stress. His doctor prescribed anti-hypertensive medication. He was still smoking and drinking heavily.

So, who did he lean on in times of adversity? Nanda remained a bedrock. 'I simply could not have done what I did without Nanda behind me. She's always been there by my side. There's nothing quite like that sort of undying support and love; it got me through many tough times.'

He would ring Rex Shore in moments of despair as well. He would sound exhausted, saying he wasn't sure if he could go on for much longer. All Shore could say was that he just had to keep going, because what he was doing was absolutely right. (Shore stayed working in Nepal on a modest retainer for more than 27 years before retiring to Australia. He had dedicated most of his working life to what he called 'The Cause' and the man he called affectionately 'Dr Sahib' or 'respected doctor'.)

Ruit continued to find great strength from two Buddhist teachers in particular: the late 3rd Jamgon Kongtrul and Gyalwang Rinpoche. Both had come into his hospital seeking help for some of their blind monks. Both had arrived quietly, without any fanfare. Both were deeply moved as they watched him work, and by the compassion he showed the poor. They invited him to their temples, to give him their blessings and empowerments.

Unlike his father, Ruit did not do formal practice by sitting at a shrine, or saying mantras and prayers with his wooden prayer beads. His approach was more one of integrating one of the central Buddhist principles—being of benefit to others—into his everyday life. Ever since his sister Yangla had died, Ruit had been determined to make a difference in the world. Bringing high-quality medicine to the people who needed him the most was his way of doing that.

For Ruit, the best part of the trips was coming home. Right from the start, he was determined to balance his professional and personal life by spending quality time with his family. Ruit's family were still living in their cramped apartment under his father's home near the Bagmati River. The living room was 3 x 4 metres, and next to it was a bedroom with two beds; one for Nanda and Ruit, and another for the children. In 1991, two years after Sagar was born, Nanda gave birth to a girl, whom they called Serabla, or 'Sera' for short. They were overjoyed with their good fortune. Five years later they had another daughter, Satenla. They were to live in that small space for almost 20 years, so that Ruit could save his money for the outreach camps.

Ruit used a small alcove off the main room as his study, just large enough for a small desk, a small television, and all his medical textbooks. Upstairs was a kitchen they shared with Ruit's parents, and the bathroom was outside. The concrete balcony overlooked a petrol station and the stench from the pollution from the river was often so unbearable in the late evenings that they had to shut the windows, making it swelteringly hot and dark.

'It was already a small place, but, as the children grew up, space got very tight and it started to feel more like a storeroom than an apartment. We were really feeling a bit pressed in,' Ruit admits.

By the mid '90s, when the camps were in full swing, Sagar had grown into a curious five-year-old, eager to explore the world. He was the apple of his mother's eye. Three-year-old Serabla charmed them as she pranced about the house, telling them make-believe stories.

Every evening when he came home from work, Ruit would scoop them up, give them both a big hug, pat Serabla on the head, then sit down with them, and ask them about their day. After dinner, they would watch television, or play Carrom Board, a billiard-style board game played throughout Asia.

Returning from an eye camp or a conference abroad, Ruit's smile would be even wider. 'He would be like a big glowing mountain when he walked back in after being away for a week or so,' Serabla recalls.

Nanda would cook his favourite curry or roast dinner and the children would follow him around the apartment, peppering him with questions about the trip. What had he eaten? What were the people like? Where had he stayed? He'd always bring them back gifts—cars and train sets for Sagar, and dolls and soft toys for Serabla, and, later, Satenla.

For many years, while they were living in such cramped confines, the young family would treat themselves to a weekend at Hattiban, a picturesque mountain resort about an hour out of Kathmandu. Ruit and Nanda would sit on the lawn under the trees, enjoying curries for lunch, taking in the view of the Himalayas, and watching the children play on the swings and slides. They all loved the sunshine and space.

Saturday afternoon was the one afternoon of the week when Ruit did not work. It was completely quarantined for his family. Work colleagues might be invited to their flat, but it would always be a noisy family affair, with everyone's children invited. They'd scream with laughter chasing each other, playing hide and seek and tag.

Ruit would often bring the children to Pullahari monastery when he worked there, too. They would play with the young 4th Jamgon Kongtrul, the reincarnation of Ruit's guru, the 3rd Jamgon Kongtrul. It was a treat to run wild and free in the garden of tropical flowers, perched high on a ridge above Kathmandu.

10

SECOND CHANCES

What many people don't realise is how cripplingly lonely life for a blind person can be in a country as poor as Nepal. Like everyone else, the blind yearn to be useful, for people to talk to them, to be part of the ebb and flow of village life. It's usually easy to find the blind when you arrive at a village. They are the ones who are hunched over, their faces etched with worry, staring vacantly at the ground or the floor in front of them. It doesn't take long for depression or mental illness to set in, especially those who are left alone for many hours of the day.

Just ask Kamisar Tamang, a woman Ruit met at one of his eye camps. Accompanying the surgeon on the trip was Australian journalist Catherine Marciniak whose documentary *A Himalayan Vision*, 1991, captured the grim psychological effects of being trapped in darkness for years.

More than two decades later, Marciniak still recalls how shocked she was when she interviewed Tamang outside her small stone hut in the mountain village of Trishuli.

'There is often this romantic vision of the blind being looked after by their extended family. Tamang's family had given her enough food to survive, but the harsh reality of subsistence farming is that every member of the family needed to pull their weight. Tamang was incredibly lonely and depressed. She had been blind for years, and lived in an isolated little hut high above the village, and had pretty much been abandoned by her family and friends. No one visited her. Life went on in the village without her.'

As Tamang sat forlornly on her doorstep in her patched clothes and bare feet, she admitted to the filmmaker that she wanted to die. At first, she explained, when her husband left for Kathmandu to work for months at a time, one of her sisters-in-law would visit her every day. But, gradually, the visits grew more and more scarce. No-one visited her.

'She used to be nice to me, but now that I'm blind, she tells me how useless I am,' Tamang said, her face cast downward as the camera rolled. The documentary shows Tamang's utter helplessness and dependency on others; time moved slowly as she spent her days cooped up inside her small house, and she was unable to work and take part in village life. She grieved for her old life. Her independence. Her old self.

'For eight months, I haven't been able to move anywhere. I've had to stay around the house. I'm blind and I can't do anything. I haven't got any money, and I haven't got anyone to do things for me. One day I was very hungry and thirsty, I tried to get something but I couldn't walk around. So, I just sat and cried. I cried all day.'

At night, Tamang dreamed of being able to see again. She dreamed she was free to enjoy all the things she used to when she could see clearly. She dreamed she was walking on the slopes of the mountain in the sunshine, and standing among the trees she loved. Each time she woke, the reality that she could not see the world anymore was a crushing disappointment.

Like many people who live in remote areas of Nepal, Tamang's suffering was compounded by the belief that her blindness was a curse, a karmic retribution for something she'd done wrong in the past.

'Why is this happening to me?' she said. 'I haven't done anything bad in my life. I haven't been greedy. Now I just feel like crying. The local spiritual leader had told me that some bad people in the village had put a curse on me. They told me to kill a chicken, so last year I gave him 21 chickens and also some goats.'

Tamang's life was finally lifted out of the darkness after she was brought into a field surgery Ruit's team had set up on the dirt floor of the nearby village schoolhouse. The surgeon examined her eyes, which had been ruined by cataracts, and told her husband that if he could bring her to the Nepal Eye Hospital in Kathmandu, his wife would be able to see quite well again. Tamang was terrified. Rumours still circulated in rural villages that eye doctors sometimes removed their patient's entire eyeball, but something about Ruit must have convinced her otherwise.

Kamisar Tamang was a proud, determined person, and she wanted her life back. She was sturdy. And independent. She took a deep breath and started planning her trip to Kathmandu with her husband. 'I just want to get my eyes fixed. When I come back I want to farm my land,' she said.

Marciniak, like the rest of the film crew, was moved by the sight of Ruit restoring sight to as many people as he could each day at the camp. In her diary, she wrote: 'Like a scene from an epic biblical movie, over a thousand people came down from the surrounding mountains, the blind led or carried by family and friends, expecting miracles. And, the miracle of modern medicine is what Dr Ruit and his team delivered, over and over again.'

Meanwhile, Tamang's journey into the light was about to begin. Her husband gently strapped her bird-like frame into a large basket on his back, and took her to Kathmandu. After tying his wife in tightly with rope, he clambered down the rocky mountain paths for about 50 kilometres to the bus station and then caught the bus into the big city. Tamang was so nervous when she arrived at the Nepal Eye Hospital that she vomited in the courtyard. Ruit immediately calmed her down by telling her she would not feel any pain, and that he was going to give her 'in-built spectacles'—a layman's term for intraocular lenses.

As usual, Ruit listened to romantic Nepalese and Indian music in the background as he worked. (At first, he would listen via a small radio, then later through his iPod). One of his favourites was the Nepalese singer Narayan Gopal. 'I always operate to music. Always. It soothes me. And it creates a nice atmosphere in the theatre.'

And, as always, he was barefoot, allowing him complete control of the pedal under the table that pulls focus on his microscope. 'Barefoot is always so much better. You have such a better feel. It's much more tactile.' He operates barefoot no matter where he goes, even at medical conferences, and when abroad. 'At first people used to raise their eyebrows, but now they know it is my way and no-one questions it,' he says.

By this stage, Ruit had built up his stamina to the point where he could sit at his surgeon's table, doing one operation after the other, without a break, stopping neither for a drink nor a snack or even to go to the bathroom, for more than seven hours a day.

Turning up to the operating theatre day after day and tackling an enormous case load had not only refined his technique—fine-tuning 'the system', as he called it—but it had built his endurance.

What is he thinking about when he's operating? 'Mainly I'm doing a form of meditation, where I clear my mind and give the person lying in front of me my all. I give my total concentration to the patient before me. All I'm thinking about is how much I want their life to benefit from the time I spend working on them. Everything else just falls away. I can't think of anywhere else I'd like to be when I'm working, because I have built up a great team and a great system that makes me look forward to work. Going to work remains a joy, and then a great family means I look forward to going back home.

'Most of the time I get into a rhythm, and I feel comfortable and calm. There are not many things that distract me. Once in a while, if I've got a very serious pressing personal problem—for instance, if someone in my family is going through difficulties—a thought might enter my head.' So, what does he do when that happens? His mental toughness kicks in. 'I close my eyes and don't think about it. I don't go there until I've finished my work for the day. There are no distractions.'

During operations like the one he did on Tamang, he says, he is 'looking at much more than the vision of one eye. It's more of a lifesaving procedure. The magnitude of what I'm doing makes me extra careful. Every operation is an enormous opportunity to change a person's life.'

Ruit talked to Tamang as he operated on her. 'I like to talk to my patients as I go. I tell them that everything is fine. That they don't need to worry. There's going to be no pain and it's going to turn out very well. I think of how I would like to be treated if it was me lying on the table. I know I would not like to hear a lot of people making a lot of noise in the background. So, I ask my staff around me to keep the discussions to a minimum. Then I usually give the patients a little touch on the head and after I've finished the operation I tell them I've finished and that everything went well. I think partly it's because I was a patient myself as a boy. I remember how frightened and alone I felt. Sometimes, when I'm doing big numbers, it's not absolutely possible to talk for very long, but I do always try.'

The next day, Ruit gently unwound Tamang's bandages and began to show her the world again. She simply could not contain her joy when Ruit brought her husband to her and said, 'Do you know who this is?' She opened her eyes slowly, and held onto Ruit's elbow as if to steady herself. Her husband tenderly brushed her hair off her face and said, 'Can you see me?' Her smile lit up the room. As her line of sight expanded, Ruit pointed outside to the banana trees. 'Can you see out the window?' he asked her. 'What kind of trees are they? Can you see the other side of the village?'

Ruit's grin was as wide as Tamang's. He started giggling

along with her as she realised the enormity of what had just happened.

'One of the great things I have earned over a period of time is the faith of my patients. It is my biggest treasure, besides my family. A beggar on the street, or a farmer from the mountains, won't come to sacrifice an eye just like that for surgery without asking around about me. They would check me out through word of mouth. All I know is that so many people have unparalleled faith in me. I really think this is a treasure that I'm going to keep for a long time until I die. It's this faith that comes even from beggars that motivates me. Faith is very important.'

Tamang started laughing with the nurses, especially when Ruit told her she could throw away her walking stick. One of the first things she wanted to do once her eyes had begun adjusting to the light was to go shopping. She browsed through the nearby market the next day, gazing at the richly hued scarves and shawls on display. She chose a green cardigan and began her journey back to her village, this time unaided, with her husband by her side.

Sadly, it was not to be the homecoming she'd fantasised about. Tamang had been completely excluded from her village's activities for years and had lost contact with neighbours, and it showed in the lack of response when she returned. She talked bitterly about the way she'd been treated by them when she was blind, and declared she wanted to return to Kathmandu.

'Because that's where people have been kind to me,' she said. 'My parents weren't as kind as the Nepali doctor who made my eyes [work]. I pray to the gods to watch over him.'

11

THE WILD WEST

Ruit and his team tried to be as discreet as they could, but word soon spread about the miraculous results he was achieving at his cataract camps. In Nepal, they started calling Ruit 'The mad doctor curing blind people in the mountains'. The camps, they said, were 'The Wild West of eye surgery'. In the West, some eye doctors scathingly dubbed Ruit's practice as 'litigation-free surgery', implying that he was using the Nepalese people to experiment on for his new technique.

Ruit and his team were, by definition, true outlaws, performing advanced surgery without any form of regulation or a clinical trial. But by 1990, a groundswell of support for Ruit's work had begun to strengthen and grow. The eminent American surgeon Alan Robin, an associate professor at John Hopkins University in Baltimore, who had been donating corneas and intraocular lenses to Ruit for years, began documenting the remarkable results of his field work.

The *Archives of Ophthalmology* (today known as *JAMA Ophthalmology*), the magazine of the prestigious American

Medical Association, published an article by Professor Robin showing that the long-term results of lens implantation in rural Nepal were just as good as those in Western hospitals. The article put Ruit on the map—and it created a furore.

'What I wrote,' recalls Robin, 'was that Ruit was achieving the same sort of results in remote camps with the most basic equipment as patients could expect to receive at Harvard or John Hopkins Hospital in the US.' He still has some of the letters fired off to the editor saying that what he'd written was total rubbish, and that Ruit must be fabricating the data. A lot of people simply could not accept that a Nepalese surgeon with minimal resources was achieving such extraordinary results in one of the poorest countries in the world.

Professor Robin wasn't the only American expert to begin championing Ruit's work. In 1995, another well-known American ophthalmologist, Professor Alfred Sommer, from the John Hopkins Bloomberg School of Public Health, went even further by stating that what Ruit was doing was not only defensible, but that to perform any operation apart from intraocular implants would be malpractice.

'Those articles did a lot of good. They really legitimised what I was doing,' Ruit says.

Fred Hollows, too, really started to respect Ruit for the results he was getting doing intraocular lens surgery at the remote camps. Hollows and Ruit had talked a great deal, often over a late-night whisky, about their vision of providing high quality surgery to every person, no matter how rich or poor, or where they lived. But now Ruit was actually going out and doing it. He'd turned their dream into a reality.

Ray Martin recalls, 'He started to see him in a new light when he went out on his "barefoot doctor" campaign'.

Hollows couldn't believe it at first when Ruit rang him to tell him about the results. Hollows told Martin he thought what Ruit was doing was 'f--king amazing' and soon began accompanying him on the camps.

Several Western surgeons began joining Ruit on his cataract camps, as well as Hollows. Ruit was always pleased to have them on board. 'There were people in the West, similar to Fred, with good hearts, who wanted to help us. Working with us helped their careers as well, when they went back home. So, it was a win-win situation all round.'

Dick Litwin was one of Ruit's early patron saints. Litwin used to tell him, 'Sanduk, if there are any mistakes on this camp, you tell everyone they are my mistakes.' Despite the fact that there were few mistakes—Ruit estimates only 1 per cent—having someone of Litwin's calibre onside gave him the imprimatur to keep going.

Western surgeons such as Dr Litwin were prey to the afflictions of rough conditions, especially at high altitudes. Everything seemed so primitive. In the West, eye doctors were starting to use sophisticated techniques such a phacoemulsification which broke up the cataract with an ultrasound needle. Yet here they were helping Ruit out in the remote countryside, using the most basic of equipment.

Before Ruit found cheap portable microscopes, his team operated with loupes, a type of magnifying glass that jewellers use. When it was cold, these would fog up, and the surgeons couldn't wipe them because they were trying to keep their hands sterile. If they *were* lucky enough to have a microscope, often the motor that helped it move up and down to focus wouldn't work. Or the power would cut out in the middle of an operation, and the nurses would have to hold a torch so the doctors could finish the job.

Often, doctors had respiratory problems or gastroenteritis. Litwin used to say, 'Anyone can do this when they're not sick.' They just muddled their way through, as best they could.

Despite all the ailments and discomfort, many of the Western doctors who helped at the camps regard it as one of the most life-affirming experiences they had ever had. When they looked up, and saw a queue of blind people standing anxiously in line, nervously clutching their paperwork, knowing this might be the only chance they ever have of modern eye surgery, they knew they could not possibly stop.

They were operating on patients who were totally blind in both eyes, so the results were astonishing. These were not Westerners who needed to read and drive at night. They were mountain people who needed to be able to look after their children, tend their farm, and not fall off the cliff, and Ruit and his team were well able to give them a second chance.

Litwin was deeply impressed by Ruit's simplicity of purpose. 'I'm not sure if he was just born that way, or if it was because his sister had died from tuberculosis, but it was clear he really wanted to do something to help and he had met some remarkable people along the way, such as the 3rd Jamgon Kongtrul, who had really guided him, and whose advice informed everything he did. There was no doubt that Ruit had a rare quality. He was a monomaniac, obsessed with just one goal in life. He'd wake up every morning and think about how many blind people they could cure that day.'

Litwin was amazed that they could do so much with so little. The sutures, a special needle with the thread forged into them so there's no bump when the eye is sewn back up, were often used four or five times each. What was left over was sterilised with alcohol, and then used again.

Begging, borrowing, scrimping and saving for equipment had become a way of life for Ruit, and he eventually found small portable microscopes to take on the camps: $6000 Konan microscopes from Japan rather than $40,000 ones from Germany or the United States. 'They were small and sweet and did the job,' he says.

The camps, held in natural catchment areas in the country-side, slowly metamorphosed into a series of district clinics. If patients kept turning up at a particular camp several years in a row, Ruit would organise for a doctor to work there in a full-time clinic. They became part of his network of care spreading across Nepal.

On the last night at an eye camp, a big bonfire would be lit, and everyone would sit around drinking and dancing. If the camps were in safe places, Ruit adored having his family with him. By the time they were in their teens, Sagar, Serabla and Satenla were usually busily employed as volunteers; they'd help do the vision testing before the operations, and enter the patients' information on their laptops.

Serabla regards attending the camps as one of the best parts of growing up with her father.

'They were always more like community events, or a festival. It was always magical when we took the bandages off and the patients could see again. I'll never forget one patient, a woman, who had walked six hours to come to the camp, who had been blind for more than ten years. When they took her bandages off and she could see again, she said she felt like she'd come out of a deep sleep. That's what it was like for so many of them.'

12

FOR ALL THE
WORLD TO SEE

At home in the mountain villages of Nepal, Ruit's fame continued to grow. At one camp, at a village called Tupche, in the south-west of Nepal, Ruit told Shore, 'I will pray to Buddha that we have patients.' He needn't have worried: there were hundreds of patients waiting for him at a tumble-down school. Others were outside clamouring to get in. To Shore, it was like a biblical event and the scenes he witnessed were like miracles.

The sense of joy when the bandages were unwound on a group of 200 patients is still fresh in the mind of Australian actor and filmmaker Joel Edgerton.

Edgerton recalls witnessing 'an incredible scene' when he travelled with the doctor to an eye camp in northern Nepal. 'The camp was in the simplest of circumstances, just a simple schoolhouse, and the patients had walked for days along treacherous roads to get there. They were bent over by the sheer weight of their work and the elements.'

After helping several old ladies to Ruit's operating table,

he watched in astonishment, when, the next day, Ruit took off the patches over their eyes, and he asked one of them, Geeta, to reach out and touch Edgerton's nose.

'After she'd playfully tweaked my nose, it was clear she could see fingers, then faces, and then, eventually the mountains and trees around her. In five minutes in a crappy little cement room he had literally turned all these people's lives around. I will never forget the smiles on their faces, and on Dr Ruit's—his was the biggest. It was just such a celebratory atmosphere. The pleasure he receives every day helping people see again keeps him wealthy in his spirit and soul in a way he never would have if he'd spent his life doing corrective surgery in a private hospital in Dubai.'

As Ruit and his team grew in confidence, they went further and further afield. His growing reputation helped him to attract professionals to work with him and travel to parts of the world that he called 'hubs of blindness', which were difficult to access. He was never deterred by how far he had to travel, or what the conditions would be like. The simple fact was that the more blind people there were to cure, the happier he was.

The Buddhist lama in Kathmandu, His Holiness Gyalwang Drukpa, invited Ruit to work in Ladakh, a high-altitude camp in the mountains of northern India. Ruit leapt at the chance to do thousands of surgeries in a new area. Later, in Singapore, he met Tan Ching Khoon, who, through his charity, A New Vision, gave Ruit and his team the green light to restore sight throughout Indonesia and Myanmar.

It seemed nothing would stop the maverick team. No road was too far, too steep, or too high. At Gucho, in Tibet, Ruit's team managed to perform intraocular surgery on the roof of the world—5000 metres above sea level. Altitude sickness does strange things to the hardiest of men, and Ruit's team were no exception. Up in that thin air, most of them were short of breath. Ruit was beset by splitting headaches and nausea, as well. Sterilising the equipment took hours because the high altitude meant the water took a long time to reach boiling point.

'When you're up that high, everything feels like it's in slow motion. I was doing surgery, but at about a third of my usual pace,' Ruit recalls. He nearly froze to death; he was so cold that his team had to wrap blankets around his back as he did the operations. He had to keep rubbing his hands to keep them warm enough to use the equipment.

Staying in a simple country inn and sleeping on hard wooden beds on thin mattresses meant sleep was hard to come by. 'Sometimes you're not feeling your best. You feel terrible. But when you look at the type of patients you are treating, and results you are going to get, then you really feel good. It's worth the effort.'

In the early days of their outreach camps, most of the toilets were foul-smelling public areas; to avoid them, Ruit and his team would get up early and relieve themselves somewhere in nature. In Tibet, they had to contend with roaming mastiff dogs, as well. Trained to fight in battle by jumping on riders and knocking them from their horses, these wild dogs bailed up Ruit's team one morning near Mount Kailash on the way to their morning ablutions. 'We were absolutely terrified,' Ruit recalls. 'We stood stock-still and tried not to make a noise. Eventually, a herd of sheep distracted them and they ran away.'

Many of Ruit's patients at these high mountain camps of Tibet were nomads, dressed in tattered *chubas*, a type of long woollen gown, that were only washed once or twice a year. Their faces were caked black from the dust and smoke of their campfires. They were so dirty that Ruit and his team had to wash the patients' faces several times with soap and water before they attempted surgery.

Although old-style eye surgery had been done in Tibet, until Ruit arrived with his team, modern intraocular surgery had never been undertaken. Many of the patients had been completely blind in both eyes for more than ten years, so the results of Ruit's operations caused a sensation. Officials came from China, curious to see his work with their own eyes. 'They thought we were doing some kind of magic. They just could not believe we were doing it properly,' says Ruit.

TIME magazine writer Tim Blair was captivated by the reaction of the Tibetan patients. 'The duration of their misery is staggering, considering the swiftness of the procedure,' he wrote in 1999. 'Just 50 years ago, the treatment would have been a crude form of surgery known as couching . . . [it] removed the clouded part of the lens but provided no replacement, meaning that although vision was improved, it remained blurred . . . Watching them regain their sight is beautiful to behold. At first, only vague outlines of nearby objects can be seen. After a day or two, patients are able to focus on things farther away, and to make out the faces of children and grandchildren sometimes never seen before. Within weeks, their fully healed eyes can once more take in Tibet's icy, sun-reflecting landscapes. And, on a clear day, Mount Everest.'

A young Sanduk
(back row, second
from right) at
St Robert's boarding
school, Darjeeling.

Sanduk's little sister, Yangla.

'Soulmates'. Ruit and Fred Hollows in Nepal, 1985.

Ruit and Nanda
exchange wedding rings,
26 January 1987.

Ruit and Nanda on their extended honeymoon in Sydney, 1987.

(Left to right) Gabi holding her daughter Anna-Louise, Nanda holding her son Sagar, Ruit with Cam Hollows, Rex Shore and Fred Hollows holding Emma Hollows.

(Left to right) Ruit's father Sonam, his daughter Serabla, his mother Kasang, and on his lap, his second daughter Satenla. (Photo Michael Amendolia)

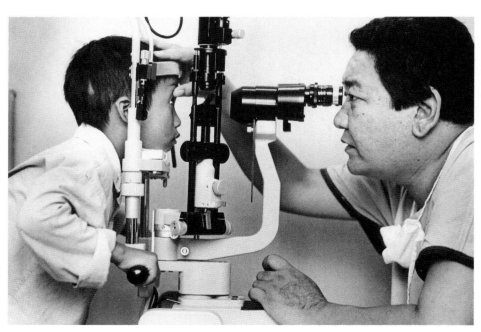

Examining Tran van Giap in Hanoi, 1992. (Photo Michael Amendolia)

Ruit's team crossing a river in Mustang, 1992. (Photo Michael Amendolia)

Ruit with an ecstatic patient, Mustang, 1992. (Photo Michael Amendolia)

Ruit operating in a makeshift
surgery in Mustang, 1992.
(Photo Michael Amendolia)

Ruit with US surgeon Dick Litwin, Mustang, 1992. (Photo Michael Amendolia)

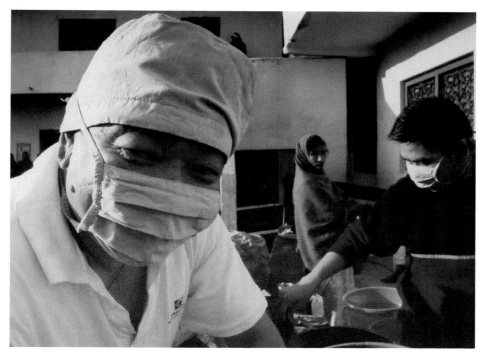
Scrubbing up before surgery. (Photo Rex Shore)

Taking a break with Australian Ambassador Les Douglas in Mustang, 1992. (Photo Michael Amendolia)

Hollywood actor Richard Gere visiting Ruit at the Tilganga Institute of Ophthalmology, Kathmandu.

Ruit's patients regard him as a God in Tibet, 1998. (Photo Michael Amendolia)

A corneal transplant by the
Bagmati River, Kathmandu.
(Photo Michael Amendolia)

The Tilganga Institute of Ophthalmology, Kathmandu, 2011. (Photo Michael
Amendolia)

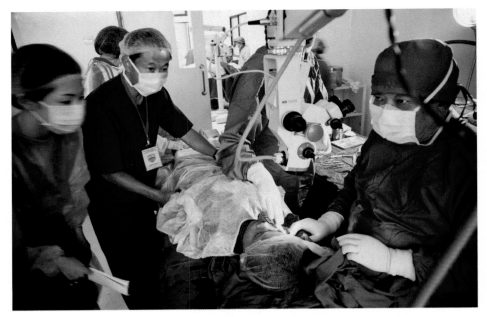

Ruit restoring sight to a nine-year-old boy in Indonesia. (Photo Michael Amendolia)

With The Himalayan Cataract Project's Dr Geoff Tabin in eastern Nepal. (Photo Michael Amendolia)

On a family trekking holiday near Mount Everest. (Left to right) Ruit, Satenla, Nanda, Sagar and Serabla.

The Hollows and Ruit families, Kathmandu, 2014. (Left to right) Rosa Hollows, Serabla Ruit, Nanda, Satenla Ruit, Ruit and Ruth Hollows. (Photo Michael Amendolia)

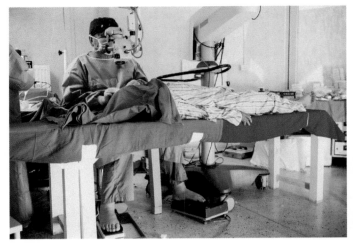

Operating in his famous barefoot style in Ladakh, Northern India. (Photo Michael Amendolia)

Examining patients in Myanmar with former Fred Hollows Foundation CEO Brian Doolan. (Photo Michael Amendolia)

A Muslim patient gives prayers of thanks for his new vision in Indonesia. (Photo Michael Amendolia)

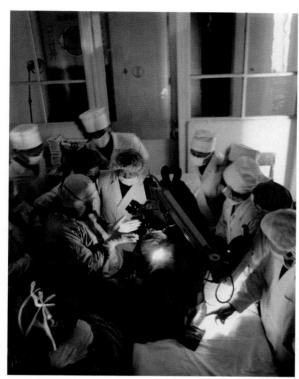

Ruit training surgeons in
Pyongyang, North Korea.
(Photo Michael Amendolia)

A patient cries with happiness after Ruit has given her the gift of sight in
North Korea. (Photo Michael Amendolia)

Thai Princess Sirindhorn at an eye camp in Lumbini, Nepal. (Photo Serabla Ruit)

On the road in Bhutan, 2016. (Left to right) Serabla, Ruit and the author. (Photo Ronald Yeoh)

Bhutan, 2016. (Left to right) Dasho Palyor Dorji, Ashi Saritri, Princess Ashi Kesang Wangmo Wangchuk, Her Majesty The Queen Grandmother, Princess Beatrice of York, Ruit and Mei Wen. (Photo Michael Amendolia)

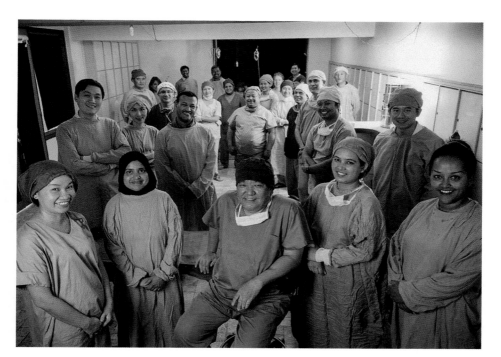

Training surgeons at Pullahari Monastery, Kathmandu, 2014. (Photo Michael Amendolia)

Ruit's supporters Mei and Chiu Chi Wen just before a patches off moment in Hetauda, 2017. (Photo Michael Amendolia)

Dr Reeta Gurung, CEO of The Tilganga Institute of Ophthalmology.
(Photo Michael Amendolia)

At home in Kathmandu.
(Clockwise from top):
Sagar, Satenla, Ruit,
Nanda and Serabla.
(Photo Michael Amendolia)

So impressive were the results, Ruit was invited to return to Tibet by an organisation run by the son of a former Chinese leader, Deng Xiaoping. Ruit seized the chance and went on to train more than 25 Tibetan doctors, as well as perform thousands of surgeries.

For sheer physical hardship, though, nothing topped Ruit's trip to Mustang in 1992, the hidden kingdom tucked between Nepal and Tibet. The medieval time capsule had been cut off from modern life for centuries. Entry had been forbidden for decades; unknown to most of the world, it had been the base for Tibetan rebels trained by the CIA to fight the Chinese in Tibet in the 1960s and '70s. In 1992, Nepal's new democratic government decided the time was ripe to open the fabled land. 'I knew the inhabitants were extremely poor and would have never been to a hospital, or seen a doctor, let alone have been able to buy a pair of glasses. I was champing at the bit to work there,' he says.

Unfortunately, travelling to Jomsom, Mustang's administration centre, instilled a terror of flying in Ruit that he still suffers from. The airport is one of the most dangerous in the world. The only time planes can land safely is before 10 a.m., when the fierce winds of the Kali Gandaki Gorge abate for a short while. Otherwise, the planes are buffeted about too wildly on their approach for the pilot to land.

Despite the fact that their 18-seater Twin Otter flew in on a calm, clear day, the wings were still so close to the sides of the narrow valley that Ruit felt he could almost reach out and touch the mountains. He was literally hanging onto his seat as they descended onto the short runway. With him were a band of his true believers: Dick Litwin, Beena Sharma, Australian photographer Michael Amendolia, and Les Douglas, who was the Australian ambassador to Nepal from 1989–94, and his brother John Douglas.

After disembarking, the team reeled back in horror. At the end of the tarmac, in a nearby creek, lay the incinerated, upside-down wreck of another small plane that had attempted to land in bad weather a week earlier.

On that same trip, they received the devastating news that a Pakistan International Airline (PIA) airbus had crashed into a cloud-covered hill of Kathmandu, killing all 167 passengers and crew on board. On board flight PK–268 from Karachi was one of Ruit's university colleagues, Rupak Sharma, the captain of the national soccer team.

'I still have to close my eyes when I'm in the air because of that trip to Mustang,' Ruit admits. 'Most of the time when I'm in a plane I am counting the minutes until we can land.'

Then it was time for the next challenge: getting to Tsarang, where they would hold the eye camp. In front of them was the 20,000-metre Annapurna range covered in snow and ice. They were about to start making their way up through some of the most treacherous mountain passes in the world, through the back of the Himalayas up to the Tibetan plateaus. Their mode of travel? Tibetan packhorses with hard wooden saddles covered in carpets. This was not a trip for the faint-hearted.

As they set out, the cold wind tore at their clothes, and the dust swirled around them, forcing them to tie cloths over their mouths to protect them from the grit. The harsh sun meant they also had to wear sunglasses against the glare.

It was three days' ride. There were no trees or grass. The

barren landscape was strewn with animal skulls and bones. Eagles soared and kites whistled eerily overhead. No-one said a word as they clip-clopped slowly along the edges of the canyon under a dark brooding sky; a sobering silence had descended as they realised just how arduous the journey was going to be.

'Mustang was a personal turning point for me,' Ruit says. 'I realised there's a limit to how far you should go to reach patients, and that I really needed to stop taking unnecessary risks. I felt a terrible sense of responsibility taking my team into such a dangerous place. I wondered what the hell I was doing. I was scared of flying, of riding horses, and heights, and here I was dealing with all three at once. Panic ran through me every time my horse's hooves came close to the edge.'

On their first day, as they wound their way past giant cairns of stones, carved with the Buddhist blessing *Om Mani Padme Hum*, Ruit silently said his prayers. He knew any misstep could be potentially fatal. He was about to find out later that afternoon when his packhorse stumbled and he was thrown off, tumbling down the slope, head over heels, so many times that he lost track of which way was up and which way was down. He plummeted about twenty metres and his horse landed right on top of him. He was bruised, scratched and disorientated when he got up, but, luckily, his fall onto a gradual terraced slope meant there were no broken bones.

'As I dusted myself off, I realised how lucky I'd been. I could so easily have been thrown off the cliff into the gorge below, rather than against the wall of the stone terrace.'

When the party had reached 13,000 feet later that day, Litwin started suffering from altitude sickness. His lips turned blue, and he felt light-headed. 'Altitude sickness is terrible when you get it; your brain can swell up and you can actually see bleeding in the back of the eye as the optic nerve swells. You get a bad headache and nausea. It's one of the occupational hazards of our work,' Ruit says.

Then it was head nurse Beena Sharma's turn. Suffering from vertigo, almost involuntarily, her feet refused to carry her around the bend of some of the narrow paths, if she so much as peeked down into the steep gorge below. 'I've never been so frightened in all my life,' she recalls. 'I'd follow Dr Ruit anywhere on earth, but on that day I just couldn't seem to go on.' Sharma had to turn back, with the aid of a guide.

The journey was like travelling back into another century, and Michael Amendolia took reel after reel of photographs of the patients they encountered. Using his favourite Leica and Nikon cameras, he was electrified by what he called 'biblical' scenes unfolding in front of him. Ruit had first met Amendolia in Hanoi, Vietnam, in 1992, when he was training surgeons on behalf of Fred Hollows. The photographer had been sent by an Australian newspaper to document the story in Hanoi. Ruit was impressed with his world-class photographs and unassuming nature. 'I loved his passion for his craft, and his gentle smile. I knew right from the start we would work together for a long time.'

Many of the locals at Tsarang spoke Tibetan. The men wore rough coats made out of goatskins and fur hats. Their faces were weather-beaten, almost black. Their body odour was so strong that Ruit and his team could smell them coming from afar. The women wore traditional tunics of blue, red, green and yellow stripes, and their hair in long braids. The children came out to stare at them curiously. Most made a living as subsistence farmers and life centred around the fire; as there were almost no trees, they collected yak dung as fuel instead.

Ruit was used to improvising, but the next town they operated in, Tsarang, took his ability to make-do to new heights. Their horse handler acted as the interpreter.

Without Sharma as his usual nurse, Ruit had to rely on his camp leader, Nabin Rai. 'I had to keep slapping his hand because he was doing the wrong thing all the time,' Ruit recalls.

The operating table had one leg missing, so Les Douglas and his brother John, being salt-of-the-earth Australian country blokes, set out to see if someone could split a tree for them. The whole place was so barren, they probably found the only tree. As there were no nails, John used wire and twine that he'd packed at the last minute at his sheep and wheat farm in Australia.

Despite the hardship, Ruit was in his element. He treated 225 people and performed 55 intraocular lens implants on the trip. 'I loved every moment of it,' recalls Ruit. 'The terrain is so rugged, that, without sight, their world had shrunk to their home, and often just their bed. These patients were absolutely ecstatic to have their sight back.'

The king of Mustang, who came down to meet Ruit at Tsarang on his white stallion, bearing a 22-calibre rifle, was so impressed with Ruit's work that he invited the team to lunch at his castle in Lo Mantang, the medieval walled city a few hours ride to the north.

Les Douglas remembers the trip as if it was yesterday. 'I don't think anything in our wildest imaginations could have prepared us for this city. We had to keep pinching ourselves.

A group of riders came out to greet us, with great Tibetan horns blowing. They were very rugged, with Mongolian-looking faces. We were right on the border of Tibet, so they were literally close cousins to the Tibetans. They rode with us to the city's huge wooden doors. We tied our horses up and were led inside. The whole thing felt like a dream.'

On a tour of the king's castle, after being offered thick yak butter tea, they were greeted with huge Tibetan mastiff dogs on the top floor. They lunged at Ruit and his team, snarling and straining from their chains. Everyone turned pale at the thought of one of them breaking free and mauling them to death.

In Mustang, Ruit and his team witnessed the ancient phenomena of a sky burial. The king's lama took them to watch the corpse of a 70-year-old monk, who had died the night before, being cut up and fed to the vultures.

Watching it left Les Douglas thunderstruck. 'When the smaller vultures were finished, the lama's assistants crushed the monk's bones up, mixed them with yak butter, and demolished the whole corpse except for the skull. Then, all of a sudden, these birds got all fidgety and flew away, and this enormous black vulture circled slowly down and finished off the monk's corpse. It was one of the most amazing things I've ever seen in my life. The whole trip with its spectacular windswept red and orange cliffs, and eagles soaring above, and shepherds in goatskins making their way toward the camp gave us an insight into what Tibet was probably like before the Chinese occupation,' Douglas says. 'It really was untouched, like some sort of lost Shangri-la.

'The whole trip was fraught with danger. Ruit almost died, Dick Litwin had shocking altitude sickness, Beena had to turn back because of vertigo. The challenges just seemed to bring out the best in Ruit. He was scared of flying, scared of heights, scared of horses, but he overcame all his fears to be able to cure blind people.'

On their trek home, staying in a goat herder's hut for the night, they witnessed the most euphoric reactions by patients. They were warming their bellies with lentil soup and local beer, when, all of a sudden, the door flew open and in came three imposing, wild-looking goat herders. They had long hair, grimy goat and wolf skins as coats, and their body odour overpowered the room.

One of them walked toward Ruit, hugged him tightly, lifted him right off the ground, and carried him around and around the room, dancing a jig. Ruit was so shocked he was speechless. He had operated on the goat herder's mother the day before and now she could see with perfect vision. It was the first time the mother had been able to see her son for more than a decade.

Their elation evaporated on the way home, however, which proved as dangerous as the rest of the trip.

Ruit had saved several lives outside the operating theatre, and one of them was Les Douglas's on the return journey. Douglas dismounted from his horse to look at the view and failed to see another packhorse bolting toward him from behind. Ruit, ahead on the road, could clearly see the horse running and shouted out. Just in the nick of time, Douglas took a step back from the edge, narrowly avoiding toppling into the steep gorge below.

Douglas's eyes gleam as he recounts the time in 1999 that Ruit also revived his wife Una's son (by her first marriage).

Zac, who had been put into a controlled coma after contracting encephalitis, was fifteen years old at the time and the couple were beside themselves with terror. The doctors in Canberra, Australia, where they were living, had told them there was a risk of brain damage.

When Ruit arrived at the airport and heard the news, he hardly said hello. He just said, 'Where's Una?' and then said he wanted to go to the hospital where Zac was straight away. He hugged Una, and just sat down next to Zac and held his hand.

'I don't really know how or why it happened,' recalls Ruit. 'But next thing I knew, I was saying to [Douglas and Una] that Zac was going to be all right. Maybe it was my patients. All the patients I had worked on, hundreds and thousands of them. Something of their energy came and took my hand and it went into Zac's system.'

Zac wasn't supposed to wake up that day, but, the next thing everyone knew, he was awake, and soon feeling well. Douglas and Una were overjoyed. They still regard it as one of the most powerful moments in their lives. 'It still makes our hair stand on end whenever Una and I think about it,' Douglas says.

When Ruit and his party arrived back in Kathmandu, they were sporting beards and had not washed for two weeks. The red dust of Mustang had permeated their clothes, hair, food supplies, cameras and suitcases. He almost kissed the floor when he walked back into his apartment.

'I remember the relief that flooded my body when I saw Nanda and Sagar and Sera's faces. I realised how valuable my life was. I vowed from then on to take better care of myself and my team.'

There were to be fewer life-threatening treks on Tibetan packhorses, and fewer flights into the world's most dangerous airports. He had a hospital to finish. Thousands of patients' sight to restore. Children to raise. His life was too precious to take risks like that again.

Professor Alan Robin was incredulous about the hardships Ruit and his team were prepared to face to reach their patients.

'Everybody has probably met two or maybe three people who have changed their lives, and Ruit was one of those for me. I can't think of anyone who faced such problems with infrastructure, politics and geography and yet who did so much to cure the blind.

'Ruit reminded me of Steve Jobs in the sense that he refused to accept the status quo, the system that was already there, and instead listened to the people and decided what they really needed, then provided it for them.'

He likes to compare Ruit's work with the work done by India's Aravind Hospital, which also restores sight to hundreds of thousands every year for free. Even the most remote rural areas in India have electricity, roads, buses, and, today, patients who have mobile phones. In Nepal, by contrast, the roads were almost non-existent; even today, there are power cuts throughout the day and many villages where there is no telephone system at all, let alone mobile phone reception.

And there was Ruit, helping blind people to see with the worst of equipment, for no cost.

To steady her nerves when he was away, Nanda would go in the early morning to light butter lamps at the feet of the three large Buddhas at Swayambhunath, Kathmandu's most famous temple. She went early, before dawn, when it was filled with devotees performing their prostrations, and saying prayers on wooden prayer beads or *malas*.

Despite her own misgivings that Ruit was sometimes in physical danger, and a long way from home, and especially before the introduction of mobile phones, Nanda remained supportive.

'It must have been really hard for her, not knowing if I was okay or not,' Ruit says. 'There were weeks when there was absolutely no way we could communicate. I knew she was worried. Sometimes she would say quietly to me, "Enough is enough." But she never stopped me going.'

'I would just light the butter lamps and remember him,' Nanda says. I would pray that all the operations would be going well. And that he would return home safely to us. I knew he would always come back.'

Another person who prayed for Ruit's work was the Dalai Lama.

In 1990, Ruit received an invitation to meet His Holiness in Bodhgaya, northern India. He regarded the meeting as the greatest accolade.

As his career flourished, Ruit's faith in the dharma, the teachings of the Buddha, deepened. The 3rd Jamgon Kongtrul, in particular, had empowered Ruit's work by reassuring him that restoring sight was just as important as chanting mantras and saying prayers.

'A few teachers told me very clearly that my work is the work of Avelokitasvara [the Buddhist god of compassion],' Ruit says.

That thought, however, did not stop Ruit being completely in awe of His Holiness. Ruit took his parents with him on the trip, and visited the sacred hot springs of Sikkim, renowned for their medicinal value, as well as the famous Bodhi tree where Gautama Buddha obtained enlightenment.

On their way to His Holiness's office, they noticed Hollywood actor Richard Gere listening to the teachings. Ruit's nerves grew as His Holiness's secretary invited him and his parents into the inner sanctum.

'As a religious and spiritual leader, he really is such an inspiration. I have great reverence for his teachings, the way he lives, and the way he inspires so many people. He influences so many people with his positive thinking. As soon as he enters the room, you realise there is a definite presence, an aura,' Ruit recalls. His parents, in a natural expression of devotion, began prostrating.

Their scheduled five minutes turned into a 30-minute audience. His Holiness's personal assistant tried to finish the interview twice, but the Dalai Lama was fascinated by the technical details of eye surgery, and how it transforms the patients' lives. Ruit told him that the state-of-the-art surgery needed to be taken to as many places as possible, to reach as many patients as possible, and that he needed to train as many doctors as he could. 'That's a very good idea. Exactly! Good impact! You should definitely do that,' His Holiness replied, giggling.

Ruit then bowed to him, and said, 'Please bless me, Your Holiness.'

He said, 'You already have my blessing.' He reached out and held Ruit's hands. He'd never felt hands so soft. He felt as if he was soaring, and something had drained out of him, almost as if he had entered another world. The Dalai Lama's touch was like receiving an electric current or volt. It was as if his batteries had been being completely recharged. His Holiness remains a steadfast supporter. Since that initial blessing, the Tibetan Buddhist leader has continued to endorse the eye doctor's work, and to offer his assistance in any way he can, particularly with his outreach camps and his work in Tibet. 'Dr Sanduk Ruit is a man from a humble background who has made the most of opportunities offered to him and dedicated his life to the well-being of others,' the Fourteenth Dalai Lama says. 'His life and work embody real altruism in action . . . Dr Ruit is driven by the conviction that everyone with treatable blindness has a right to have their eyesight restored, and that problems and solutions transcend geographical boundaries.' As for Ruit, he continues to regard Tenzin Gyatso's blessing as a form of empowerment, vastly increasing his capacity to help others through his work.

13

FAREWELL TO A FRIEND

Business was almost non-existent for the few years of Ruit's small private practice in New Road. Hardly anyone sought him out. He didn't even have his name on the door.

'I used to call it "catching flies", sitting there in the evening, doing nothing, just waiting for patients to turn up,' he says.

But by the late 1980s, Ruit's reputation had grown so much that there was a long waiting list to see him. Patients travelled long distances to go under his knife.

The French Buddhist monk and writer Matthieu Ricard, who had been bringing monks to him for treatment, was so impressed by Ruit's surgical skills that he arranged for his 93-year-old mother to fly into Kathmandu. 'Everyone said, "Are you crazy? You want your mother to be operated on in Nepal?" But I already regarded him as the greatest artist in the world when it comes to operating on cataracts, so I told my mother I would definitely prefer [she have it done] in Kathmandu rather than in Paris,' Ricard says. 'When we got back to France, her doctor said, "Wow, this is impeccable work!"'

When Swiss-French public health expert Dr Nicole Grasset, known as 'Mother Teresa in a Dior dress', needed cataract surgery, she refused to see any other surgeon than Ruit. She flew all the way to Kathmandu from Geneva for Ruit's finesse.

But, just as Ruit's career was about to take off, his world came crashing down around him. In 1992, he learnt the devastating news that Fred Hollows had terminal cancer. Ruit was at an eye camp at Nuwakot, a picturesque village about an hour north of Kathmandu. Film maker Catherine Marciniak took him to one side as the team sat around the fire one evening, enjoying a drink. She pulled her chair up close. 'Dr Ruit, I'm sorry to tell you this, but Fred has been diagnosed with cancer.'

Ruit sat there in stunned silence. Hollows had been having treatment on his kidney when his surgeon discovered he had cancer that would probably spread quickly to his lungs. There was nothing really that could be done to control it. Each word felt like a physical blow to Ruit's chest.

His mind was reeling. Hollows was only 62. He had smoked all his life. But why did he have to go now? They had so many plans: building an intraocular lens factory, and a new hospital, for a start. They had such a long way to go together.

'He and Gabi were my surrogate family. I felt I wouldn't be able to continue on with my work if Fred was not there. I wasn't sure how I could go on. My sister Yangla had died far too young—that was devastating—but the news that Fred was dying too now came as such a terrible shock. I was devastated in an entirely new way.'

Ruit rang Gabi when he got back to Kathmandu, deeply concerned about her.

'I knew she wasn't working and the children were still so little and needed her so much.'

Hollows had been Ruit's mentor, teacher, champion and brother.

Over the years Ruit had tried to emulate Hollows, by learning to speak up about the things that mattered, having more confidence in himself, and, most importantly, inspiring confidence in others.

'Fred had an incredible charisma, and a capacity to inspire others with a desire to help carry out his dream,' says Ruit.

'He was very direct. He would say, "If you don't do it this way, I'll kick your arse," but he was usually right. He was such a deep thinker on all sorts of issues, especially anything to do with public health.'

What Hollows taught Ruit was that it *was* possible to do something in public health that made a difference. He had drummed into his protégé that countries in the developing world like Nepal had to learn to do things themselves with the money they received in overseas aid, rather than rely on fly-in, fly-out foreign expertise. Hollows was always outraged that so much of Nepal's foreign aid money went back to the First World in the pockets of Western doctors. He scornfully called these doctors 'medical tourists'.

'All they want to do is a bit of work at the hospital before they go on their holiday trek in the mountains. What long-term good does that do?' Hollows would bark furiously. Nepal had to learn to stand on its own two feet. What the West should be doing instead, he said, was to 'Give them a fishing rod, teach them how to fish, and then piss off.' What he meant by that was that he and Ruit needed to set up hospitals and train as many local doctors as they could, so that they could continue his work—long after their biological lives had ended.

Ruit and Hollows saw each other twice before his death. The first time they travelled to a surgical camp in south-west Nepal after Hollows' kidney was removed. He had to be propped up with pillows in the four-wheel drive during the long, bumpy road up out of Kathmandu Valley. The last time they saw one another was in Hanoi, Vietnam. Hollows had promised the government of Vietnam he would teach intraocular lens surgery there, even if it meant taking an oxygen mask with him.

In June 1992, after a seven-hour operation, Hollows pulled the tracheotomy tube from his neck, bandaged the wound, and discharged himself from hospital. A week later he met Ruit in Vietnam.

Using the most basic equipment, the pair held an eye surgery workshop in Hanoi's old communist hospital. Hollows was too sick to operate, so Ruit did the bulk of the 107 procedures, and Hollows oversaw the 60-odd operations undertaken by Vietnamese trainees. He stood behind the doctors saying, 'Do it this way' or 'Do it that way.'

He tired easily and used his oxygen mask a lot. 'I was really shocked when I saw him,' Ruit says. 'He'd lost so much weight and he was really struggling, he was trying to speak through his tube, but he couldn't speak properly. It was just so sad to watch someone who had been so robust needing all these devices to stay alive.'

Within days, the pair had shown the trainees how to perform the fast, affordable, delicate new technique Ruit had perfected.

'I think they felt more confident because I was someone they could relate to,' says Ruit. 'They had a notion in their head that this is a surgery only a white person could teach. It was unthinkable at the time, but, there I was, this misfit from Asia, doing the operations in seven minutes rather than 45 minutes as the French had been doing. And showing them that they could do it too.'

The results the next day, when the first batch of patients had their bandages unwound, left the young Vietnamese surgeons thunderstruck. 'When they saw the first ten or so patients seeing so well again, they could hardly believe it. From that moment on, the ball was in our court. They were in awe.'

That initial training program went on to revolutionise eye care in the country, making Vietnam a world leader in the fight against avoidable blindness. In 1992, a mere 1000 modern cataract operations were done; today, more than 200,000 are performed each year.

One of the patients Hollows and Ruit operated on that year was Tran van Giap, a nine-year-old who went blind in his right eye after a piece of glass accidentally lodged in his cornea while he was playing with glass tubes.

Giap was the youngest and brightest of six children and on the threshold of starting school. It was a cruel blow for his whole family. His father, Tran Duc, made the expensive trip to Hanoi, 170 kilometres away, seeking treatment for his son. They waited for about three weeks, only to be told there was nothing that could be done. They were just about to turn around and go back home to their village when Hollows and Ruit turned up.

Listening to music and humming a little as he operated,

Ruit worked on the youngster the next day. Hollows and Ruit changed his life. Instead of having to stay at home to help his mother in the garden or his father in the rice field, Tran van Giap was able to go to school, study and enjoy a career as a high school teacher. A photograph taken by Michael Amendolia of Hollows examining Giap's eyes in Vietnam has turned Giap into something of a poster boy for The Fred Hollows Foundation; he is living proof that restoring sight changes lives. (The photograph, used during several promotional campaigns, has since raised millions of dollars for the Foundation.)

Hollows was just skin and bone and using his oxygen mask a lot when Ruit talked to him for the last time in Hanoi. 'I said, "Fred, how are you feeling?" and he said, "Sanduk, you know my days are numbered."'

Hollows gave his friend a big bear hug and said, 'I reckon we're going to have difficulty seeing each other again, mate. They're going to do some more treatment on my lungs, but I don't think I'm going to get any better. You just keep your work up. What you're doing is great. Keep going.'

For a while, after Fred died in February 1993, Ruit was plunged into a deep melancholy, as he had been after Yangla's death. He was bereft without his friend. He found it hard to accept that Hollows was gone for good, and that he somehow had to carry on without him. He was dumbfounded that this man who had lived so passionately, who had such a huge vision, and who had achieved so much, was no longer in his life.

He knew Gabi would support him, but also that she could not do what Fred could. He rang Gabi, who told him to keep going, because that's what Fred would have wanted him to do. He talked to Nanda, and confessed to Rex Shore how lacking in confidence he felt. Rex said the same thing as Gabi: just keep going, even if Fred's not here. Do it for his sake. And that's exactly what Ruit did.

Ruit had a great vision for what he wanted to do. He had the surgical skills, but, for a long time, he needed Western help—mainly equipment and funding—to achieve his vision. Ruit firmly believes that without Fred and Gabi, he would not have gone on to carry out his lofty goal. Part of Fred Hollows' spirit has stayed with him, propelling him onwards, Ruit says. His friend is still watching over him.

14

THE BEST OF MY LOVE

After their operations, Ruit's patients enter a thrilling new world in which everything is bright and well-defined. Faces, trees, food—everything about them looks fresh. Sometimes seeing the world again can come as a shock, too. Some patients are saddened by how old their relatives look, or how humble their homes are. One Laotian single mother was horrified when she returned home after sight-restoring surgery to see the dilapidated hut she had been sharing with her children. She'd been unaware that their home was little more than a bamboo shack that was in danger of being swept into the river whenever it rained.

But usually new vision is a cause of relief, and great jubilation. One of the most dramatic physical transformations Ruit ever witnessed was that of a homeless old woman brought into their annual clinic held at Kalimpong, northern India. The woman looked like she'd just been dragged out of the gutter. Her face was battered, her skin was shrivelled, she was stooped over, and her few clothes were almost in tatters. Her gnarled, rickety legs and worn feet were almost blackened with dirt and she smelled as if she hadn't washed for about a year. 'The people who brought her in told us she would sit in the corner of a lane and wouldn't eat for days,' Ruit says. 'She slept in the corner on a sack and was half demented. Sometimes she would hit the wall and shout. She had no family or friends to speak of.'

Ruit usually only does one cataract at a time, with several weeks in between. But this woman was so unbalanced he doubted she would come back for the second one, so he did both the same day. The nurses showed her the tap and gave her a towel and some soap, so she could wash her face and hands, then gave her something to eat and drink. The day after her operation, they gave her some new clothes: a sari, a pair of sandals, and a white cardigan. She couldn't stop crying when she saw them laid out neatly in front of her. Were they really for her?

She asked for a few rupees to buy a small plastic comb. Someone brought her a mirror, and the first thing she did was arrange her hair into a bun. She had been miserable for so long that she'd forgotten how to smile. She had to practise pulling the muscles on either side of her face upwards in front of the mirror. Soon after, she took up a loan to set up a small grocery store.

When Ruit returned to the same eye camp a year later, he noticed a new grocery shop that had been set up nearby and sent a boy over to buy sweets for the youngest patients.

The owner wore a soft pink sari, pretty earrings, and her dark hair was swept elegantly off her face. Someone asked Ruit if he remembered her.

He was perplexed. Had she been a school teacher to one of his children? A nurse at his hospital? Eventually, the boy said, 'Don't you remember? You operated on her last year at the eye camp.' They used to call her 'The mad woman of Kalimpong'.

'I couldn't get over the change in her, she was like a new woman. Work doesn't get much more satisfying than that, does it, when you can do that for a person,' Ruit says.

At another of Ruit's camps, a seventeen-year-old boy was brought in by his mother. He was so hunched over, so curled up in himself that Ruit's team thought he was either physically or mentally disabled. His mother said he had been so bright, and wanted to be a teacher or a doctor, but that he'd had to leave school because he couldn't see the blackboard. The boy had railed against his fate, kicking the walls inside their stone hut. His mother despaired of him. Rather than being able to watch him grow into a young man who could go to school and make his way in the world, he had become just another mouth to feed. Ruit operated on both his eyes for cataracts.

When his eye patches were unwound, the boy had uncurled from his foetal position and stood up straight. He came out of his shell, he started talking and exploring his surroundings, he scrambled to the top of a pile of rocks to take in the view. His mother just couldn't stop smiling. At last, her son had a chance of going to school and making something of his future. It was like watching a chrysalis burst into life.

Despite the fact that he has operated on more than 120,000 people, Ruit still finds himself holding back tears as he watches his patients set out on the road home, without having to hold someone's hand or the hem of their shirt.

'When I watch people seeing their loved ones again, and returning home independently, I cannot put my feelings and emotions into words,' Ruit says. 'All the money in the world would never give me the same sense of fulfilment and achievement.'

Ruit may give his patients the gift of sight, but they give him a great gift, too; the opportunity to witness such an incredible transformation. He has enjoyed this privilege almost every day for more than 40 years. He says if he gets the chance to be born again, he would definitely choose to be an ophthalmologist. 'Patients often come up to me and say, "You are like a god to us," but the truth is, it is more that they are like a god to me. They are the reason that I gain so much joy from my work,' says Ruit.

'During the operation, I am giving them the best of my skills and all of my love. And then experiencing all those complex feelings in the room when the patients realise they can see—the relief, the joy, the tears, the hugs, the jubilation of seeing their children, their parents, their brothers and sisters again—is always such a powerful moment. It really keeps me going. The rewards are just so rich.'

15

LITTLE RIVER

Ruit fantasised about building a new hospital. The one he held in his mind's eye was precise. It would be three storeys high, surrounded by a garden. Its foundation would be rock solid, built with three or four times the normal amount of steel and concrete used in Nepal in order to withstand earthquakes. It would outlive him, and his children.

The operating theatres would gleam with the latest technology, and the spotlessly clean waiting rooms would be bathed in sunshine. Ophthalmologists would fly in to learn from Ruit from every corner of the world, before being set to work in the world's blindness trouble spots.

An eye bank would be set up for corneal transplants. Inside the front gates, a shaded courtyard with benches and clean drinking water would greet patients. A factory would manufacture intraocular lenses for a fraction of the price of those made in the West, making them affordable for everyone.

That was his vision. Ruit was also painfully aware that, in Nepal, building sites were easy targets for unscrupulous middlemen and corrupt contractors; tips and bribes—known as 'tea money'—were a way of life. Ruit knew Hollows was sceptical about breaking away and building a new eye hospital. The words 'brick walls' and 'construction' seemed to equate with 'empire-building'.

But Ruit was prepared to build it brick by brick with his own hands if he had to.

He is a firm believer that if your motivation is right, you meet the right people at the right time. When Ruit first met Les Douglas in 1989, they liked each other immediately. As the Australian ambassador to Nepal, Douglas was a straight-talking, no-nonsense man, renowned for rolling his sleeves up and getting the job done. He'd previously been posted to Japan, Myanmar and Switzerland, but it was in Nepal that he became more involved in his career than ever before.

Douglas saw the value of what Ruit was trying to do and was prepared to use his position to knock down doors to get the hospital and the intraocular lens factory built. He could see how committed Ruit was. 'He had such a vision. He outlined that it would not be plain sailing, and, I don't know what it was, whether it was a unique quality in him, but I knew I had to do everything I could to help him.'

Like most processes in Kathmandu, building a hospital was a bureaucratic nightmare. Shore would zoom about on his 100cc motorbike with 'NEP' written on the petrol tank, visiting the endless list of officials from whom they needed to obtain building permission. Even the most straightforward steps seemed to take months.

Meanwhile, Douglas was flexing his diplomatic skills to persuade Prime Minister Koirala to grant Ruit some land on which to build his dream. Every week, Douglas and Shore would troop out to the surveyor general's office. The surveyor general would bring a dusty old map of the city, dating back about 70 years, out of a metal cupboard and unroll it on the table. The three of them would pore over it, looking for unwanted tracts of land. Each time they found something, they were told it was already taken. 'Usually, it was someone in the royal family, or a friend of the royal family's or the prime minister's. It was unbelievably exasperating,' Douglas recalls.

Finally, they found a parcel of land they thought no-one would probably want, on the banks of the Bagmati River. Slightly downstream from Pashupatinath temple, the Hindu holy site where cremations were held on wooden funeral pyres, the quarter of a hectare was overgrown with weeds and surrounded by slums. It stood empty for the entire year apart from every February when thousands of Hindus thronged into the city for the Shivaratri religious festival and it was used it as a parking lot for buses.

When construction commenced in 1991, Douglas became so involved in the building of the hospital that Shore and Ruit called him 'H.E.'—short for 'His Excellency'. He was at the site every day, making sure the concrete was poured perfectly, and every beam was as straight as an arrow. He'd often take a carton of beer down to the site for the workers when they'd finished for the day. He even asked for his tenure as ambassador to be extended for eighteen months in order to see the hospital finished.

Ruit has always been gifted at visualising. On long drives out of Kathmandu into remote villages, lulled into drowsiness by the motion of the four-wheel drive, he will gaze quietly out the window for long periods of time, or his eyelids will start to droop.

It often looks like he's dozing. What he's really doing is a form of meditation he calls 'visualising with the third eye'.

He completely quietens his mind. 'I try to empty myself of everything, from the top of my head, out to the tips of my fingers and toes, to create a vacuum. Then out of this base level of absolute quiet comes the power to come up with useful innovative ideas for my long-term vision,' he says. He regards these times of deep introspection and insight, as his most precious and personal moments. 'They're wonderful, very constructive,' he says.

But even Ruit's legendary visualisation powers were tested to the limit that first morning when he went out to look at the site. Dogs picked their way through the weeds, cows wandered through the rubbish and broken pottery. The din of Kathmandu's incessantly beeping tuktuks, cars, trucks and mopeds filled his ears. Smoke and ash from the funeral pyres drifted across the river from Pashupatinath.

Despite flowing past the holiest of Hindu shrines, the stench of the river was so overpowering that it was impossible to stand next to it for long. The ashes of the dead weren't the only things tipped into the water. Dead animals and rubbish also floated down the river.

It was one of the most desolate spots in Kathmandu. But standing there, the day the land was signed over to the Nepal Eye Program, was one of the great turning points in Ruit's life. Finally, he had land. It was going to be an almighty task, but, brick by brick, he was going to turn the rubbish tip into one of the finest hospitals in the world.

He decided to call the hospital the Tilganga Eye Centre, Tilganga meaning 'a stream of sesame seeds' or 'little river' after the small stream that ran through it. He loved the sweet, simple sound of it.

There were no strategic plans. Ruit and his supporters simply had an innate confidence that things would work out.

'I didn't tell anyone except Nanda, but we didn't even have enough money to finish the foundations when we started building. It was all done on a wing and a prayer. It probably wouldn't have got through all the red tape, and would not have happened at all, if we were trying to build it today.'

Douglas's brother Brian, an architect, designed most of the hospital from Australia. Plans for the lens factory were drawn up by The Fred Hollows Foundation in Sydney, which Fred and Gabi had founded together in 1992 in order to continue his work.

The labourers started pouring the concrete for the foundation in July 1991. This took almost three months. They built double-cavity brick walls, twice as strong as those usually used in Kathmandu, using bricks of the highest grade of cement. Sixty-five labourers and bricklayers went to work, using bamboo scaffolding, and carrying the sand, gravel, cement and bricks in baskets on their backs.

Ruit's opponents, especially the doctors who worked at the existing Nepal Eye Hospital that had been treating the blind in Kathmandu since it opened in 1973, were outraged that he was building a second eye hospital in the city. They were jealous of his success, and threatened by his vision. 'They said it would be disruptive to the community,' says Ruit. 'Others called me demented, and crazy. I'm not one to raise my voice, but Les Douglas had raging arguments with some of the senior ophthalmologists who were opposed to the new hospital. He kept telling them they should cooperate with me rather than trying to obstruct me.'

Douglas held his ground.

But as the hospital slowly rose from the ground, Ruit's health began to deteriorate. He felt worn down by the constant stress of overwork and delivering results. His insomnia kicked back in, and his blood pressure shot through the roof. Nanda and Ruit had also just had their daughter Serabla.

He was put on anti-hypertensive medication, and has been on it since. He was a smoker. His family were still living in the dingy, cramped apartment near the hospital, with one bedroom, a combined kitchen and living room, and an outdoor bathroom. He used to smoke on the bed as he was reading or doing his work. It wasn't until Nanda was pregnant with Serabla that he finally stopped. Nanda pointed to her belly and said, 'You are giving this smoke to me, as well as our child.' That was the last cigarette he ever smoked.

Ruit was also still drinking far too much for his own liking. 'I picked up some bad habits after I'd graduated from medical school. I drank every day, for many years.'

He started to slide dangerously close to being an alcoholic during those years as the hospital was being built. Every day seemed like a marathon. As well as running as many eye camps as he could, he continued running his own private practice in the evening, as well as administration for Tilganga. There were also business dinners he needed to attend in order to raise money.

The drinking he most enjoyed was quiet, companionable socialising with two or three friends. It was very easy for them to finish a bottle of whisky, especially in the days that Hollows was there. 'I never drank until the afternoon and it never affected my surgery,' Ruit says. A British friend taught him how to sober up in the morning with a cold shower, and an Alka-Seltzer, with cold water and a drop of lemon.

Things came to a head for Ruit when he attended a party for a friend of Tilganga's chairman. He had done about 70 back-to-back operations that day and was enjoying unwinding over a whisky. 'Then someone gave me a gin, then a beer, and on and on it went until I simply wasn't aware of what I was drinking at all. I must have left the party half-conscious and, somehow, by the grace of God, I made my way home.'

Nanda was furious. She refused to let him inside. 'Coming home at your age in this state, it's just embarrassing,' she told him. 'You're making a complete fool of yourself.' Her words hit home. He apologised and stopped drinking from that day onwards.

He had terrible cravings for about a month, but since then, he has not touched a drop. He admits to eating too much, and that he was addicted to marsala tea for many years, drinking it all day long, especially the way Nanda made it, with milk, cloves, cardamom, cinnamon and lots of sugar. These days he's even given that up too, and drinks endless cups of tea with lemon and honey tea instead.

Fundraising was not Ruit's forte at all, but Douglas was a master of the art. He was not only charming and likeable, he was totally committed to seeing the hospital and the intra-ocular lens factory built. He had lines of communication going right up to Prime Minister Koirala, and he was not afraid to use his connections to make things happen. He was very persuasive.

'This hospital is going to be a role model for our whole country,' he'd say. 'It's really going to put Nepal on the map.' The decision makers and influential businessmen of Kathmandu soon became used to the sound of Douglas's voice. When the prime minister dragged his heels approving the latest plans, Douglas would knock on his door and say, 'Look, we really need some decisions to be made.' Douglas and his wife Una would hold elaborate fundraising parties at their home and the Australian embassy. They lobbied every-where they went. Douglas persuaded Australia's foreign aid investment, AusAID, to donate $70,000.

And they lobbied whomever they met. Over lunch one day, the Australian entrepreneur Dick Smith asked Douglas and Una, 'How can I help?' 'A hundred thousand will do,' Douglas instantly replied. The next morning, Dick's wife Pip rang and asked, 'Where do you want the hundred thousand sent?'

The Nepal Eye Program Australia donated $30,000, and several wealthy Nepalese businessmen donated signifi-cant sums. An unexpected windfall came from the Jamgon Kongtrul Foundation, which donated $71,500—enough to build the new operating theatre.

When the 3rd Jamgon Kongtrul first turned up for surgery, Ruit thought he was 'just an ordinary monk who happened to be very smart'. He had no idea of the Rinpoche's status.

'When we realised he was actually a high lama—there were hundreds of monks prostrating themselves before him—our team made a small presentation at his temple, asking for funding through his charity. In retrospect, it was all quite amateurish, but within a few days, they'd offered twice what we'd asked for—enough to pay for the entire theatre.'

A month before the hospital opened, Les and Una Douglas and Rex Shore took a driver and a truck up switchback roads to the nurseries above Kathmandu. They returned with an abundance of camellias, bottlebrushes, avocado trees and flowers for a small army of volunteers to plant in the hospital's garden. The date had been set for the opening of Tilganga: 7 June 1994.

16

OPEN FOR BUSINESS

Kathmandu usually begins to swelter under hot and humid days in the middle of the year. The blanket of pollution from the thousands of tuktuks, motorbikes and trucks clogging the streets starts to choke the city as the monsoon season approaches. But 7 June 1994, the day the Tilganga Eye Centre opened, dawned gloriously clear and bright. The temperature was 24 degrees and, in the distance, you could see the snow peaks of the Himalayas.

Inside the hospital, Ruit was pacing the plain brick corridors, fraught with nerves.

Hundreds of people had gathered outside the hospital to watch King Birendra of Nepal (who reigned from 1972 to 2001) and Prime Minister Koirala turn up. The two were arch enemies, and this was the first time they had ever appeared in public together. Early that morning, workmen at Tilganga had knocked down a three-metre-high brick wall in front of the hospital they had only built the previous day. Ruit and his team suddenly realised that so many people were coming that they would need extra room for a big marquee for the guests.

Ruit's nerves were quavering at the thought of the daunting task before him: performing live surgery in front of the huge crowd. The display, which magnifies a surgeon's microscopic moves on a giant screen outside the operating theatre, is regarded by eye doctors as the Olympics of eye surgery.

'It's very scary,' says Ruit. Even those at the top of their game avoid it if they can.

Australian ophthalmologist David Moran, who was at the opening day on behalf of The Fred Hollows Foundation, describes it this way: 'When you're doing live surgery, every shake, every wobble shows, and woe betide if you screw up. Eye surgery is a craft which imposes a brutal honesty on its practitioners. Nothing can be hidden. It becomes obvious for everyone to see, as quick as a flash, and all in real time, if you've made a mistake. You have to have nerves of steel and a very healthy ego to be able to do it.'

Ruit tried to have a good sleep the night before his ordeal, and a light breakfast—fried rice, an egg on toast and a cup of tea. Coffee was out of the question.

The fact he had to perform on opening day, in front of everyone he knew in Kathmandu, including every one of the city's dignitaries, made the pressure excruciating. 'It really felt like the eyes of the world were upon me,' he says.

Ruit felt as if his whole life—all the late-night study at medical school, breaking away from the Nepal Eye Hospital, crossing rivers and climbing mountains to reach remote eye camps—had been a long, arduous preparation for this one day. He was as keyed up as a musician about to give the performance of his life.

The hospital staff were on edge, from weeks of frenetic activity making sure everything in the hospital was running perfectly. No one had got enough sleep. Even Gurung, Ruit's second-in-command, known as 'Cool-hand Gurung' for her toughness under pressure, was shaking like a leaf. Although Nepal was a democracy, the royal family were still as revered as deities. For the king to come and open the hospital meant a great deal to them.

By 9 a.m., every handrail, piece of machinery and doorknob had been polished until it shone. The foyer was fragrant with marigold flowers. The place started filling up with hundreds of visitors, as well as television cameras, newspaper reporters, and all the dignitaries of Kathmandu in their finest clothes. Nanda and Sonam watched on with a mixture of pride and terror. The head eye surgeon of Bhutan, Dr Kunzang Getshen, wore the full traditional costume: a knee-length robe, complete with belt and dagger.

Today, the reception area of Tilganga is teeming with people in need of help, crammed in together, standing cheek by jowl, as they make appointments, clutching their paper-work. But the day the Tilganga Eye Centre opened, Ruit and his team were so worried they would not attract patients that they posted staff on the nearby roads advertising 'free cups of tea with free eye surgery'.

'It's hard to imagine now, isn't it?' Ruit asks.

Every twenty minutes or so, there was an update from the Narayanhiti Palace about when the king would be arriving. 'He'll be here in one hour!' his assistant would announce; 'He'll be here in fifteen minutes!' Finally, the king arrived, in a swirl of dust in his black Mercedes. He was driving himself, and so quickly that his police escort had trouble keeping up. Gabi Hollows greeted him, looking proud and serene, along with Fred Hollows' two brothers Monty and John.

Dr Getshen presented a traditional silk scarf to the king as a sign of respect.

The late Australian author Bob Ellis reported on the opening for *Good Weekend,* his senses reeling as he rode in a tuktuk to the hospital: 'After 20 minutes of bone shaking and beeping, risk to life and limb, we arrived. There was a dirty bridge, a filthy river, two burning corpses, a number of golden splashing children, a temple carved with penises, a monk on a hunger strike and 20 hectares of marijuana growing as untended and unremarked as paspalum. Before the factory, a brick wall was being pulled down by the same Nepali workmen who had built it the day before. All of Asia, I decided, in 300 metres . . .'

Inside, Ellis noted the hospital was 'crammed with elderly blind, silent people who looked like Bible illustrations, often two together, man and wife, sometimes lying stoic on a single stretcher, holding hands.'

Ruit got to work, tackling his usual assembly line of operations, about one every seven minutes. He was absorbed in removing a particularly stubborn cataract in a female patient when the strangest thing happened.

It had been sixteen months since Hollows had passed away, but Ruit suddenly had a strong sense of his friend being there in the room, watching over him. It was at once spine-tingling and completely reassuring.

'It was as if he was just another one of the surgeons in the room. It felt like he was standing there behind me, staring at me over his mask with his hands on his hips, just as he used to. And he was saying in his grudgingly approving way, "That's it, Sanduk, you've got it. That's very good." In a way, it made total sense. I knew that he would have been so glad to see the way it came together. I was almost in tears when I finished my last patient that day,' says Ruit.

'It still makes me very emotional remembering that moment. After I'd finished all my operations for the day, Gabi, being the sweetheart she is, gave me the hugest hug. I think she'd felt Fred's presence very strongly too, and she knew how monumental this day was for me. The Nepalese don't really have a culture of hugging, but this was the warmest, most beautiful hug I could ever remember. It contained so many complex emotions. Sadness that Fred wasn't here to see it. Joy that it had opened. Relief that the big day was over. Pride in what we had achieved.'

The emotions of the opening day left indelible memories for David Moran, too. 'Ruit would have really been under the gun. He looked absolutely terrified. But like most top surgeons he would have performed the public surgery brilliantly no matter what was happening, whether there was an earthquake or if he was operating on the king—or both at the same time.

'The opening of the hospital was an extraordinary day. Ruit and his team had surmounted so many obstacles to make it happen, and he'd tackled them all. It was a day of frenetic activity and a sense of mission in the fullest sense. You don't get progress of such radical nature and rapidity without conflict. But beyond that there was a sense of everything being suffused with joy.'

Despite all the naysayers, all the people who said he was crazy, and that it couldn't be done, Ruit had done it. Just eighteen months previously, The Fred Hollows Foundation, set up the year Hollows died, had assessed the feasibility of building the hospital and had been sceptical that it could be done. But once it saw that the factory was going to start manufacturing 50,000 world-class lenses a year, and a squadron of surgeons was going to be needed to put them in, they had come on board. They raised more than $10 million for the lens laboratory, which has gone on to become the hospital's beating heart.

The Tilganga Eye Centre was open for business. Most of the staff went out to celebrate that night, but Ruit was spent. He couldn't wait to go home to be with his family.

~

The Nepalese calendar is a swirling profusion of religious holidays. Daishan, a fifteen-day-long festival in either late September or early October, is set aside specifically for family feasts during which women wear *tikkas* on their forehead (a mark made with vermilion powder). A month later, Deepawali sees fairy lights strung up over the city's temples and courtyards. Bright orange marigold flowers are festooned over cows, dogs and buses, and, night after night, family gatherings and parties linger into the wee hours.

During such festivities, Ruit would always make sure he and Nanda seized the chance to go on a small trek with their family in the foothills of the Himalayas. It was always a physical relief to climb out of the valley in a four-wheel drive, away from the hospital, and set off in his walking boots, comfortable clothes, a small backpack and his cloth cap, through the pine forests and scenic trails, and take in great lungfuls of mountain air.

Ruit is never as happy as when he's trudging uphill, giving his huge heart and lungs a workout, gazing out at the white peaks, or out over the great terraced valleys of the region, slowing down only to wait for everyone at the next teahouse.

Like his own father, Ruit has an abiding love of nature and the rugged beauty of Nepal. Taking in a view of Kanchenjunga, his home mountain, always soothes his frayed nerves or dejected spirits. His favourite season to go trekking in the foothills or mountains is in early spring, between February and April, when the rhododendron forests are abloom with blood red, pink and white flowers. 'The whole feel of the place, the smell, and the atmosphere, calms me down.'

One of Serabla's vivid memories as a girl was of her father '. . . walking so fast. He would stride along, telling me that it wasn't his body that was moving quickly, it was his mind. He used to tell me that determination was the most important thing.'

Trekking in the mountains proved to be the antidote for many of his troubles. By the time Ruit was in his thirties, he had become almost painfully aware of his own faults, the main one being his short temper. He began to realise what sort of effect this could have on those around him. His remedy was to head uphill, with one or two friends, using the silence and peace to collect himself.

'I've become more and more aware of my faults as I've gone along in life,' he says. 'I'm full of them, and still have things to learn. I have very strong likes and dislikes for instance, and if I don't like someone I show it immediately. It's very obvious to the other person. I can't even look at them. And I can be a bit thin-skinned as well. I can brood on things for a bit too long. Thank goodness I have Nanda to smooth things over sometimes,' he says.

His mood would lift with every step he took out of Kathmandu Valley. 'I always come back feeling myself again, and gain a proper perspective on things when I'm up at higher altitudes, and out in nature,' he says.

Ruit can be fierce, too. It's a side rarely seen, but it can feel like a blowtorch for the person on the other end, as some of his close colleagues can attest. 'I can be very abusive,' says Ruit. 'For example, one of our staff started having an affair. I told him he was not fit to live with his family. I told him they were too good for him, and that he could go to hell. He eventually left his job at the hospital. I don't know where the hell he is now. I'm very protective of family life. I have only harsh words for people who act immorally. Once in a while, we get a joker in our team like that, who is immediately fired, but I am blessed with 98 per cent of staff who are all exceptional people.'

Trekking was always the best salve for his other major foible as well—his love of food. Ruit has never been cavalier about his health. But after giving up drinking and smoking, food became a comfort to him; he was aware that he was carrying too much weight for his own comfort. Nanda keeps a close eye on his diet, but he still tucks in with gusto at mealtimes. Tenzing Ukyab, his cousin, diplomatically calls him a 'foodie'.

'He's well-disciplined when it comes to not drinking or smoking since he saw the toll it has on his health, but he's not where food is concerned. He loves food and can eat a lot.

He's a bit of a connoisseur. Whenever the family goes out to eat together, we most definitely leave him to do the ordering,' Ukyab says. 'I know I have to eat less,' Ruit sighs. 'It's really just the only indulgence I have left.'

17

PIECES OF MAGIC

The intraocular lens factory, which opened in 1995 as part of the Tilganga Eye Centre, was Fred Hollows' idea.

After breakfast one morning at an eye camp many years earlier, the starry-eyed surgeon suggested Ruit start making lenses in Kathmandu. Instead of being beholden to Western hospitals and doctors to donate lenses, he could make his own, and, in the process, drastically cut the price. 'All you need, Sanduk,' he said, 'is a bloody shed.'

The reality of building a high-tech factory in a country such as Nepal proved to be a lot more complicated than that, though. At one stage, Ray Avery, the New Zealand scientist and engineer commissioned by Hollows to build the laboratory in Nepal, called it 'mission impossible'.

Avery had made a name for himself as a highly successful entrepreneur, building factories for pharmaceutical companies in China, Thailand and Vietnam. But his days of high-rolling profits came to an abrupt end when he was summoned to Fred Hollows' sickbed at his home in Randwick. Hollows pointed a bony finger at Avery's chest and said, 'Stop making money out of sick people, Ray. Start doing something f--king useful with your life.'

Hollows first asked Avery to set up a factory in Eritrea. There, the odds seemed insurmountable. The country was only just emerging from a brutal 30-year war of independence against neighbouring Ethiopia. As well as losing tens of thousands of its citizens, the capital city, Asmara, lay in ruins. Avery could not find power or water for the factory, let alone new electrical cabling; he had to resort to second-hand cabling from dilapidated buildings.

Once the factory was built, he also realised, to his horror, that the Australian lathe machines needed to cut the small pieces of plastic were completely faulty. The manufacturer Hollows had chosen to make them had completely failed to do the job. 'We had dinner in a friend's house in Kathmandu that night,' Ruit recalls. 'We got drunk and started arguing about what to do.' Avery had to go back to the drawing board; he eventually found a small company based in Florida, USA, to supply new lathes.

The Kathmandu factory was just as fraught with problems, too. One Monday morning, as Ruit was halfway through a corneal transplant, someone burst into the operating theatre with bad news. An Australian electrician, Stephen Murphy, had been electrocuted installing lights at the laboratory. A live fuse had been accidentally left in the box he had been working on.

Ruit ran to the factory to find Murphy lying on his back on the concrete floor, having stopped breathing. Ruit knelt down and did cardiopulmonary resuscitation, furiously pumping his chest. The Australian didn't lose his larrikin streak, even on death's door. Looking up at Ruit's 80-kilogram frame bearing down on him as he regained consciousness, he shouted, 'Get off me! Get the f--k off me!'

To top it all off, they were about to be embroiled in a public relations scandal. The *Sydney Morning Herald* was preparing to run a scathing article that The Fred Hollows Foundation had lost half a million dollars on the faulty lathes. Mike Lynskey, the CEO of the Foundation at the time, swung quickly into damage control, assuring the journalist that not only had the problem been solved, but that they'd just completed a big sale of lenses using the new machines from Florida. The story went no further.

'It would have been a terribly anxious time for Ruit,' Lynskey recalls. 'It was a lot of work for us, but, at the end of the day, we could go back to Australia. Whereas Ruit had to stay in Nepal where his credibility was really on the line. If the intraocular lens factory [in Nepal] had not worked, it would have seriously undermined his claims that it was possible to make world-class lenses at a much cheaper price. He had a lot of opposition, he had the Indians looking over his shoulder at his every move, and he really stuck his neck out. The pressure on him was enormous. The whole idea was Fred's, but then he left us to work out how to do it. Both The Fred Hollows Foundation and Ruit took a massive risk getting it up and running.'

The risk paid off handsomely. But by the time the intraocular lens factory opened in June 1995, it was more akin to a laboratory in Switzerland than something you'd expect to find in the developing world. Inside, the air and temperature were closely monitored, the equipment was computer-driven, and the staff wore space-age-style blue protective clothing as they meticulously cut, ground, polished and sterilised the lenses that sold for $5 each compared with $100 in the West. It was the first factory in Nepal to be quality-assured with international standards. Thanks to Avery's finesse, the plant has since gone on to produce more than five million 'little pieces of magic', as Gabi Hollows calls them, which are sold in more than 70 countries around the world.

The lenses Avery produced were so good that Indian competitors and large multinationals could not believe that a product stamped with 'Made in Nepal' could be world-class. It was a classic case of David and Goliath—a small charity in Nepal pumping out world-class lenses for a fraction of the cost of the ones produced in the West.

'The big multi-nats were absolutely furious with us,' Avery says. 'At medical conferences, Indian manufacturers would stand up and shout, "You're cheating! You're trying to ruin our business!"'

'The senior executives must have been so threatened,' Avery says. 'They couldn't believe we were making these superb lenses in Kathmandu.'

'Ray Avery did such a fantastic job,' Ruit says. 'He built the first factory in Kathmandu that was quality-assured and documented. What the lens factory proved is that if you can do something like that in Nepal, you can do it anywhere in the world. The factory he built was one of the real keys to our success. We were finally able to take on the big multinationals and show the world that we could produce the same quality for a fraction of the price. We were able to keep the cost of the operation right down to the barest minimum. And we were one of the first in the world to do it.

'The factory [symbolises] that, no matter how poor you are or where you live, everyone deserves high-quality sight. The laboratory did away with the haves and the have-nots, once and for all.'

Avery is sanguine about his success. When he met Ruit, he realised he was dealing with a man of great substance. Ruit didn't pat him on the head. He had simply chosen Avery, as he had chosen his initial team, to carry out a certain task because he knew Avery was exactly the right person to do it.

Avery regards himself as a changed man after finishing the factory. He found himself profoundly moved by the thought that millions of people could now see clearly because of the lenses he helped produce in Kathmandu. He never worked for another chemical company again. Instead, he set up a charity, Medicine Mondiale, which manufactures medical equipment such as incubators for premature babies at a fraction of their usual cost for the developing world. He received a knight-hood for his philanthropy in 2011.

The factory continues to produce 600,000 lenses a year. Ruit has ambitions for it to eventually produce three times that amount. 'It's a big market—as the population ages, there will be an increasing number of cataract surgeries. The lenses will help Tilganga to become even more self-sustaining,' says Ruit.

18

LEAN ON ME

Ruit can be gruff and intimidating to newcomers. He had learnt to have his guard up against ambitious Western doctors who had professed a desire to help Tilganga, only to discover they were simply what Hollows used to call 'medical tourists'. By this, he meant doctors who wanted to chalk up a few dozen operations in the developing world on their resume before heading for the Himalayan snow peaks and a bit of an adventure.

Ruit's standards have always been dizzyingly high, and he is notoriously difficult to impress. So, at first, he hardly noticed the young American surgeon Dr Geoffrey Tabin, who had been sent to him as part of his corneal fellowship by Professor Hugh Taylor from the University of Melbourne.

In those early days, no-one would have suspected that, together, Ruit and Tabin would eventually form a dynamic collaboration. They created a charity called the Himalayan Cataract Project (HCP) in 1995. It's small but potent, punching way above its weight; the staff of eleven raise more than US$1.3 million a year to support the work of Tilganga Institute of Opthalmology, as the eye centre was later named.

But first, Ruit and Tabin had to make friends. It seemed unlikely at first, as the two got off to a disastrous start.

To say Tabin is ambitious is an understatement. Before he turned up in Ruit's world, he had not only studied at Yale, Oxford, Harvard and Brown Universities but had climbed to the top of the world's seven highest mountains. As well as bungy jumping in his spare time, he was searching for a way to make a difference in global health.

Yet, the initial impression he made on Ruit was that of a 'hyperactive jumping jack'. 'He just seemed to be unable to sit down in one place,' says Ruit. 'He made me feel giddy.' Ruit took one look at Tabin's climber's hands and told him they were too rough and the knuckles were 'too bent' for him to ever become a decent surgeon.

Tabin recalls Ruit was 'stand-offish'. 'He wasn't warm and fuzzy. It was pretty clear he was the professor and I was the student.'

He thought Tabin was yet another medical tourist who wouldn't stick around long enough to make a difference.

But Ruit became intrigued by the young doctor when he came along to an outreach surgical camp in the lower ramparts of the Himalayas. At their end-of-camp party, a Tibetan surgeon got drunk and passed out under one of the dining tables. He was a giant of a man, over 100 kilograms—so heavy that none of the Sherpas could move him. Despite being at an altitude of about 9000 feet, which makes everything a lot slower and harder to do, Tabin somehow managed to pick up the heavyweight by his feet and drag him backward into his bunk. Tabin told Ruit casually over break-fast the next morning that he had also summitted Mount Everest. Ruit took a second look at him.

He still missed Fred Hollows. And he was well aware that Western doctors gave his work real clout, and could launch his work onto the global stage. He knew how powerful the resources and advocacy of a Western business partner could be.

Tabin, at any rate, was already hooked. On that surgical camp, he had been moved watching a blind grandmother see her grandchildren for the first time in years after surgery. As the tears of joy ran down her sunburnt face, he realised he'd never come across anything quite like it in medicine.

'It was one of the most cost-effective health care interventions I'd ever seen,' Tabin recalls. 'I realised it was possible to make a permanent change for the better in their lives after one short operation. The euphoria of the patients seeing again was intoxicating.

'Watching the patients who had walked for days across the mountains, lining up at the screening tables for the chance to see the world again [were some of] the most extraordinary moments in my life. I was this brash, confident American who thought I was going to be teaching the Nepalese some-thing about state-of-the-art cataract surgery. Instead, I was the one who ended up doing all the learning. I just stood there watching in awe, mesmerised by the way everything flowed, the way Ruit and his team delivered world-class care to so many patients in such a short amount of time. My head was spinning. His technical skills were incredible. His work ethic was phenomenal. He did surgery for eight hours a day and kept directly talking to the trainee who was operating on an adjacent table. It became immediately obvious that he had truly revolutionised care for the poor.'

When Tabin returned to the United States after two weeks in Nepal, he began pestering Ruit, ringing him every few days, telling him how much he wanted to help. He just would not let go. Finally, Ruit decided to test him to see what sort of stuff he was made of.

He dispatched Tabin to a large hospital, the Golchha Eye Hospital in Biratnagar, on the stultifying hot plains of southern Nepal, near the border of India, about as far away from the romance of the Himalayas as possible. During the monsoon season for good measure, too.

Tabin arrived in a week of overwhelming heat and humidity—it was on average 43 degrees every day—with drizzling rain, and squadrons of mosquitoes. He put his head down and worked sixteen hours a day, trying to teach the resident doctors the new style of intraocular surgery, only to receive a distinctly chilly reception. At one stage, Ruit rang him to upbraid him for criticising the hospital staff. 'He really laid into me, he said, "What the hell do you think you're doing, criticising the doctors there? Your job is to improve surgery, not drive everyone away!" And then he hung up on me. It was really rough.'

But Tabin proved to be just as tenacious as Ruit. He took the point, learnt his lesson, rolled his sleeves up and continued to work from sun-up to sundown, for the rest of his six months there. 'He thought I'd go scurrying back to America,' Tabin said. But like Ruit, he was a man who was not for turning. When he returned to Kathmandu, having vastly improved the standard of surgery at the hospital as well as performed thousands of operations, he detected a flicker of approval from Ruit. Not long after that they started discussing ideas for what would become the Himalayan Cataract Project.

The charity began out of a battered cardboard box in the back of Tabin's Honda Civic outside his home at the time in Vermont, United States. Job Heintz, the current CEO, recalls Tabin handing him the jumble of paperwork amid his tennis racquets and mountain climbing gear. 'Here you go, see what you can make of all this,' he said, passing Heintz a few years' worth of tax invoices, receipts and handwritten reports. Within a decade, Heintz, an environmental lawyer, and Emily Newick, the current chief operating officer, had created a fundraising giant.

As well as an ability to attract extremely generous donors, HCP also has a flair for unlocking the lucrative coffers of USAID. In 2009, after winning a huge USAID grant of $700,000, which was matched by $1 million from American donors, the charity doubled the size of the Tilganga Institute of Ophthalmology. The 12,000-square-metre addition to the hospital included new training rooms, accommodation for trainee surgeons and a highly profitable refractive surgery for paying patients. In the process, they transformed Nepal's finest hospital into a world-class training centre. In Professor Hugh Taylor's words: 'Tabin and the HCP picked up Tilganga and took it to the world.'

Tabin, now a Professor of Ophthalmology at Stanford University in California, has become Ruit's right-hand man. He readily admits the humanitarian work is 'far more audacious than setting out to make the ascent on the East Face of Mount Everest'.

Tabin and Ruit are close, defining their relationship as 'older brother, younger brother'. Tabin is an extrovert and Ruit is an introvert. Ruit brings wisdom, expertise, and a grand vision, and Tabin brings unbridled enthusiasm, energy and fresh ideas. Sometimes zany ideas.

'Sometimes his behaviour is quite outrageous,' Ruit says. 'I remember once we were sitting down to have dinner with a minister of Sikkim [a state of India] and his officials. It was quite a formal social occasion, and the king's youngest daughter was there. She was very beautiful, and then suddenly Geoff had this lady sitting on his lap. It was completely outrageous to be openly kissing a Sikkim princess like that, even if she was his girlfriend.'

The two are guests in each other's home, and know the comings and goings of their family lives. Tabin would talk to Ruit every day if he could; Ruit manages to rein him back to once every week, if possible. 'We work really well as fantastic partners. Sometimes we might squabble, but our hearts are both in the same place. It's important to have a strong partner in the West like Geoff. Destiny brought both Fred and Geoff to me to help my work. It's a great partnership—I am hands-on, and am constantly devising new ideas to improve the system, and they have both nurtured it by helping with resources, as well as being great advocates. And [Geoff] fundraises so well. He networks with American universities—he's exceptionally good at networking with high-end ophthalmologists.'

Ruit is proud of the way Tabin has been shaped by his influence. 'Tabin has matured so much, he's become a lot wiser, and much more influential. And a much better surgeon, too.

He is someone that I feel a great pride in being able to reshape. He has moulded himself into a perfect international leadership role. He's used Tilganga's ideas of team-building, and bringing high-quality eye care to the poorest communities.'

Ruit recalls returning to the Jamgon Kongtrul Memorial Home in Kalimpong, bone-tired from a harrowing day's drive across the mountain range, only to find Tabin performing magic tricks for the orphans living there.

'He did these crazy tricks with ropes and cards and the kids were just screaming and giggling with laughter. You always know when Geoff is around.'

19

BLINDED BY THE LIGHT

Ruit always loves to hear about his patients and how their lives have turned out after their operations. A classic example is Kanchi Maya, the timid young mother brought to his eye camp who saw her baby for the first time after Ruit operated on her. A team from Tilganga recently returned from Kanchi's village to find her a changed woman. Today, she is the matriarch of her home. She makes a living picking corn from the fields with the other women, fetches water, cooks, sews, and sends her son, now a healthy eight-year-old, off to school, dressed neatly in his school uniform. She looks ten years younger, and stands taller. She greets her friends and family with a thousand-watt smile.

'Kanchi had big white cataracts and was cut off from the world. Now she's got her authority back, her place in the society,' Ruit says with a touch of pride. 'She's very much in control of the house. It's beautiful to see.

'To me, this shows how one operation can affect the whole village. If we had not been able to get to her, the results would have been tragic. The baby was so malnourished, he was close to perishing, and the mother was anaemic. The whole household rhythm had been broken. We see this over and over again, not just in Nepal, but in subsistence families and agriculture in India, Asia and Africa where we work. Blindness breaks the rhythm of the family, the whole society. When we restore sight, we restore the whole balance,' Ruit says.

'Often, they remind me of wilted plants that suddenly bloom when potted in the sun. Their dignity is restored because they can earn money or help out on the family's farm. There are no side effects of cataract surgery. There are no downsides.'

Kamisar Tamang, the woman who was once so lonely that she wanted to kill herself until her husband strapped her into a basket and brought her to Ruit, also stays in touch. She's a sprightly 70-year-old now, and whenever she comes to Kathmandu, she brings Ruit fresh eggs or potatoes. Her husband has passed away, but she's a part of the fabric of her village; she works for her brother, and enjoys looking after her nieces and nephews.

Gifts of chickens, eggs and corn, and bottled fruit from patients, are a common sight at Tilganga. For those who cannot afford anything else, they are a simple way to say thank you to the man who gave them back their sight. Ruit is always touched by the gifts, and takes them home to Nanda to cook, or gives them to other staff members. Another patient, Toprasad Sharma, likes to bring ghee and bottled pickles when he comes to Tilganga for a check-up.

Sharma came to Tilganga in the late 1990s from his village in the foothills to the north-west of Kathmandu. He was 21, but he looked a decade older. Thin and stooped, he clambered off a bus, and shuffled across the bridge to the hospital gates on a hot summer afternoon, clutching the shirt tail of the man leading him. At the time, he had nothing to his name other than five rupees in his pocket and the clothes he was wearing: a shirt, shorts and a pair of slippers.

For the previous fourteen years, Sharma had been trapped in the half-life of the blind. When he was seven, an operation at a local clinic had badly botched one of his eyes, both of which were already clouded white with calcified cataracts. His father was afraid of going to the hospital again. He was ashamed of his son, and wanted him to stay at home in the back room, away from the gaze of visitors and friends. His former school friends teased him and played tricks, such as making him trip over thorns or walk headlong into the path of a bullock. His mother's love was his only comfort, and when she died when he was seventeen, he became unbearably lonely.

His dreams of becoming a teacher had faded and he no longer went to school. Scared of falling over a cliff or into a ditch, his world shrank to the confines of his two-roomed mud home. He would spend his days sitting on the doorstep, listening to the sounds of the village around him.

'I lost all hope after that,' he says, as he tells his story in a Kathmandu cafe close to the hospital. 'I used to hear my father talking about me to his friends, saying that my life was over. It used to make me cry. The only thing I started wishing for was to die. It was the only way I could think of escaping the sadness of getting through my life.'

Finally, after a sleepless night, he decided to give his life one last chance. He would use all his money to catch a bus to Kathmandu, 24 hours away by bus. If he couldn't find anyone to cure his sight, he would end his life.

'That's easy when you're a blind person,' he says. 'You just listen for a bus or a truck and step out in front of it.'

But within minutes of arriving in Kathmandu, and asking directions to the disabled people's hostel, a stranger told him about a new hospital that was curing blind people for free. Plucking up the last remnants of his courage, Sharma took a deep breath and said, 'Can you take me there now?'

'Dr Ruit talked to me more gently than anyone else I'd met,' he says. 'He was the only person who'd ever spoken to me with such kindness. He was much nicer to me than my own father.

'He explained I had a good chance of seeing again, and that he would pay for my accommodation while I was waiting for the operation. I could hardly believe what he was saying, but I started to place my hopes in him.'

After a nurse anaesthetised his eyes, Sharma was led into the operating theatre. Ruit spoke to him gently as he made a tiny incision into the side of his lens. He flawlessly removed Sharma's cataracts, which were the size of small pebbles, and replaced them with the small plastic intraocular lenses made in the laboratory next door.

'It was the happiest day of my life,' he says of the magic of being able to see again, after Ruit unwound his bandages the next day. 'First, I looked at the doctor's face, which was even kinder than his voice. He looked like someone from the mountains, like someone from where I lived, not a typical city doctor. Then I looked out the window, and I could hardly believe what I saw. I could see the ridgeline of the mountains!

Birds! Buildings! Buses and trucks and people everywhere! The tops of the temples! What world was this I was living in? Everything seemed new again.

'Then I looked in the mirror and looked at my own face. It was amazing, after fourteen years, to see what I looked like. I was crying with happiness.'

As Sharma recovered, his world expanded. He visited all the temples in Kathmandu. He began to dream of going back to school and becoming a teacher. Almost twenty years later, every detail of those ecstatic days is vividly etched in his memory.

'When I went back to the village after the operation, my father was so ashamed that he had not sought help any earlier, and he begged my forgiveness.'

He works as a high school teacher, and has bought a house in his village for his wife and five children.

Years of blindness have given him an appreciation for the world that is sharper than most. 'I really just want to enjoy everything now in my life,' he says. 'I'd love one of my children to become an eye doctor. And I'd like to see more of this beautiful world.'

'I don't know how I can really ever thank Dr Ruit,' he says. 'For me, there is God and there is Dr Ruit, and those two things are the same. He gave me more than my sight back. He gave me my life.'

The blind are already some of the most vulnerable people in the developing world—easily abused, overlooked, neglected. Restoring sight to young women, particularly, can save them from the very worst form of exploitation. So, it was a golden moment when Ruit operated on two blind sisters, fifteen-year-old Maslia and nineteen-year-old Nurasni Nubis, at an eye camp in Northern Sumatra.

The pair had been blind for more than a decade; Maslia was three when cataracts cast a shroud over her world, and she could not see the toys in front of her. Nurasni was nine when she went completely blind and had to leave school. Their blindness was possibly caused by malnutrition, either during development in their mother's womb or as babies.

'When the patches were taken off, the sisters were holding hands, there were tears of joy everywhere you looked,' Effi Jono, the director of A New Vision, Tilganga's partner in Singapore, recalls. 'Everyone was crying with them, even the onlookers.'

The girls' father died of lung disease a year after their operation. Soon after, their mother died after suffering a stroke, leaving them with only two elder brothers, and in a vulnerable situation.

Many blind women are abused by their husbands and are unable to leave. They're trapped. Young pretty girls from poor families are already at risk of being forced into prostitution, but if they are blind, then that risk multiplies.

Today, Maslia is married and Nurasni looks after their home, and Jono keeps a close eye on them. 'The hardest thing to overcome in young women is a lack of confidence and the belief that they deserve to fulfil their dreams and have educations and careers. Women are so often told their place is at home, and that they don't need anything else to be happy. It can really hold so many young women back.'

Now they can both see, their chances are much brighter. Jono is hopeful she can persuade them to continue their studies.

20

KATHMANDU CALLING

Ruit's drive is remarkable. Somehow, against the odds, he'd managed to build a world-class hospital in the dysfunctional capital city of Kathmandu, where power and petrol shortages are a way of life, corruption is rife, and a series of self-serving governments have left the country on its knees economically.

Not content simply to restore sight to multitudes, Ruit then set up a system of training surgeons around the world in his technique. He'd built a laboratory that made intraocular lenses for a fraction of the price they cost in the West and, by doing so, had started to make a serious dent in cataract blindness. But he still needed to keep pushing on with the gargantuan task of reducing the backlog of the blind. Next on his list was stemming the floodtide of corneal damage, the second most common cause of blindness in Nepal.

During his decades as an eye doctor, Ruit had seen more corneal damage than he cared to think about. The damage was usually caused by birth defects, farm accidents and untreated infections. He was desperate to treat these tiny grape-like pieces of skin that cover the eye like the face of a watch.

As usual, there were friends from the West who were keen to help. Geoff Tabin and Dick Litwin, in particular, would try to clear the backlog by bringing in about 50 corneas a year, carefully packed in styrofoam boxes, whenever they flew into Kathmandu to accompany Ruit on the eye camps or to help at the hospital.

But Ruit knew they needed so many more corneas to start making a difference. And besides, a typical journey for one of Ruit's 'boxes of eyes', as he called them, would involve them being flown from a teaching hospital in the United States, out across the Pacific Ocean to Hong Kong and then finally on to Kathmandu. It was a ridiculously long trip—halfway around the world—for such tiny pieces of human tissue.

Things finally came to a head when Ruit arrived at Tilganga early one morning to find the hospital's best corneal surgeon, Dr Reeta Gurung, slumped over her desk, fast asleep. Corneas deteriorate quickly, so she'd had to work fast during the night grafting six fresh corneas that had arrived the night before. Something had to change.

Ruit was deeply frustrated that the Pashupatinath cremation site, a source of hundreds of healthy corneas, was tantalisingly close: just 800 metres away, in fact, from his operating theatre. But instead of being able to harvest them to graft onto blind patients, the large supply of corneas was consigned to fire every day. He despaired whenever he smelled the smoke from the funeral pyres on the river, knowing all that healthy tissue was going to waste.

Pashupatinath is one of the most holy and peaceful places

to depart the world. The only sounds are the lapping of the water, the caw of crows, and holy men reciting prayers and mantras. The corpses, wrapped in shrouds, are placed on stretchers on the ancient stone steps with their feet almost touching the river. Soon afterwards, they are carried to the timber pyres, and their ashes swept into the water. Men with shaved heads, clad in white, set tea lights afloat on lotus leaves further down the river.

Ruit would walk there whenever he could take a break, and he began to quietly approach the Hindu authorities. Would it be possible for families to consider donating their relatives' corneas before they were burnt? He was scrupulously polite, but his efforts were rebuffed every time.

'It was just so frustrating,' Ruit says. 'For the Hindu community at the time, it was taboo to donate any part of a corpse, because they thought this meant the person would be without that part of their body in their next life. No matter how passionately I explained the virtues of the act, that such a small part of the body could transform someone's life, and that it was meritorious for both the donor and the donor's family, the Hindu priests would not listen. They were fixated on the idea that we were taking the entire eyeball out. They just turned their backs and walked away from me.'

Ruit railed against their prejudice. His medical training—based in scientific logic and facts—was at loggerheads with such unbending spiritual beliefs. Surely it was of greater value to give sight to the blind with these tiny pieces of flesh than see them turned into ash?

But like almost everything else he does, Ruit was dogged. He just did not give up. Finally, he hit on a plan. He invited the head cremator at the time, Krishna Thapa, to come to Tilganga and see his work. At first, Thapa was sceptical. But Ruit encouraged him to watch several operations, and then took him to the recovery rooms. For Thapa, who had spent his life among the dead, watching the patients at Tilganga having their bandages removed, and then witnessing their euphoria when they could see the world again, was akin to a revelation.

Getting Thapa onside made a huge difference. In 1995, Ruit formed a partnership with Pashupatinath, which has gone on to restore sight to more 11,000 people, thanks to donated corneas.

What kept driving Ruit to set up the partnership was that the results, when he actually got his hands on fresh corneas, were spine-tingling. One patient he'll never forget was Mainala Gomi. Gomi was fifteen when her brother and father brought her into the crowded waiting room of Tilganga.

She had been blind from corneal damage for more than a decade. The young woman could not even walk along the street without holding onto her sister's arm for support. She longed to be useful: to go shopping for her family, to cook dinner, to finish school, and hopefully one day have a family of her own. But most of her days had been spent lying or sitting on her bed. She'd only completed a few years of school, and there was no prospect of marriage.

When Ruit unwound her bandages after her operation a few days later, and Gomi opened her eyes, everyone caught their breath. She was captivating. Her eyes were large and brown, and when she walked outside into the sunlight, they sparkled with flecks of gold. Her whole face began to shine with joy. Within a few hours, she was singing Hindu love songs. Gomi could see, and her future had changed. 'Now one day I might have a husband,' she said. 'I can have a life of my own.'

'It was such a joy to see Mainala leave the hospital in a new dress, and full of hope,' Ruit says.

A masterstroke of the corneal donation program was Ruit's idea for a team of counsellors to gently approach families, just as they were about to organise for their relatives to be cremated. The Shrestha clan was a classic example. When they brought their 80-year-old mother to Pashupatinath, one of Ruit's counsellors, trained by the head of the eye bank, Shankya Twyna, quietly made her way through the throng toward them.

The grand dame had suffered a heart attack at 3 a.m. that morning. After unloading her from the ambulance, her family burned incense on each corner of her stretcher and lay marigolds and carnations over her shroud.

With her luminous brown eyes, soft wavy hair and a pink sari, the counsellor approached the family, and, with great sensitivity, asked if they would consider donating their mother's corneas to Tilganga, just on the other side of the road. It will only take a few minutes, the counsellor explained, and there will be no harm done. The corneas will give a patient a second chance at life. The men of the family quietly conferred, heads bowed together, over their mother's stretcher.

A short time later, they nodded to the counsellor to go ahead. When the first corneas were collected by Twyna, they were taken out right next to the funeral pyres by the banks of the river. Later, excision rooms were built. For the Shrestha family, technicians from the electric crematorium set up a few hundred metres away from the river bore their mother on her stretcher into the excision room where she was transferred onto a steel operating table. Her steel-rimmed spectacles were removed, and placed on a tray. One of Tilganga's eye bank technicians went to work, removing the transparent covering of her eyes with his scalpel and forceps. He placed her corneas into a sterilised bottle, and put them in a small refrigerated box which was whisked away to the hospital.

Small plastic caps were placed over her eyes, her eyelids were closed, and she was returned to her family. The family stood around her stretcher in a circle, and their wailing filled the room. The doors to the crematorium opened, and she was engulfed in flames.

Within hours, across the road at the hospital, one of the surgeons began suturing her corneas into place on a patient. The Shrestha family's matriarch was no longer with them, but, for one fortunate person, she left the gift of sight.

The Tilganga Eye Bank now has all the corneas it needs. It sends surplus corneas around the world, from Bhutan to China, Malaysia, Pakistan, Cambodia, Bangladesh, Indonesia, Thailand and East Timor. Ruit and his team have made donating corneas as ordinary as donating blood.

21

SHINING STAR

Staying in Nepal has meant Ruit has not made a great fortune, but neither he nor Nanda have ever been particularly materialistic. All too often, they had seen specialists on big salaries who had every material advantage and yet never seemed satisfied. That's not to say there haven't been a few temptations along the way. One of the positions Ruit turned down early in his career was as the personal physician to the Sultan of Oman, which would have come with a large house, a personal driver, and a chef. A lucrative position in Sydney beckoned after their year living with Fred and Gabi Hollows. A hefty salary could have been his for the taking if he'd moved abroad to the United Kingdom or the United States.

But he looks genuinely puzzled when asked if he has any regrets about the path he chose instead. The idea of amassing the trappings of wealth such as fancy cars or expensive overseas holidays seems to have barely registered in his consciousness. He's probably the most unlikely international star Nepal has ever had. After more than 30 years on the road as an eye doctor, restoring sight still bewitches him. It's a form of intoxication that never fades. There's nothing as satisfying, apart from seeing his three children gain educations and start navigating their way in the world. 'None of them are high-flyers, they just all put their head down and work hard. We're very proud of them,' he says.

By turning his back on the trappings of materialism, Ruit had become a cultural hero in Nepal. The *Kathmandu Post* regularly features front-page stories about him receiving yet another award. Travelling with him is akin to being with royalty; hospital and hotel staff make way for him like the parting seas. The country's most influential businessmen and politicians are contacts on his iPhone, whom he'll occasionally ring from the back seat of one of Tilganga's Toyota LandCruisers on the way to the next camp.

Ruit always stayed well above politics—his own leanings are a mystery—but, by 2000, his stature in the country had grown to such an extent that he'd been asked to head several of Nepal's political parties. He always said no, much to Nanda's relief. But there was one diplomatic role Ruit was proud to perform: that of unofficial adviser to the Nepalese royal family, especially to the much-loved late King Birendra.

The surgeon had been invited several times to dinner at the royal family's home, Narayanhiti Palace. Despite the fact that he felt distinctly ill at ease, he would sit quietly through the formal five-course banquets under glittering chandeliers with the upper echelons of society. The dining room walls, decorated with giant oil paintings of former kings, and the heads of stuffed tigers, trophies from hunting expeditions, were a world away from his simple apartment and private consulting room.

'I could never work out how someone like me, with such a modest background, ended up having dinner at the palace,' he says. 'I must admit I never felt truly comfortable being there, but the king, God bless him, always tried to make me feel at ease; he would call me "Doc" and ask very nicely about my work.'

Like many Nepalese, Ruit had conflicted feelings about the royal family; he felt the country should move toward becoming a democracy, but he also adored the king.

Tilganga had become an example of what Nepal could do, beyond politics, free of corruption, and King Birendra, wishing to take the same approach governing the country, asked Ruit's advice on many occasions. He respected Ruit because he knew he was in touch with the common people.

Ruit also met the king's son, the Crown Prince Dipendra, known as 'Dippy' for his habit of breaking the speed limits in his sports cars and his penchant for semi-automatic firearms. 'He was a good drinker, much like Fred,' Ruit recalls. 'I remember how he used to love washing down Scotch whisky on the palace veranda.'

Many Nepalese regarded King Birendra as something of a demigod. He was a unifying force in a deeply fractured country, with many different ethnic groups and castes. He made people feel safe, especially during the brutal, ten-year civil war (1996–2006), which saw thousands of Maoist rebels trying to overthrow the government to alleviate centuries of poverty and suppression.

Ruit, like millions of Nepalese, was devastated by the events of 1 June 2001. Just when peace talks with the Maoists were starting to look hopeful, nine members of the royal family were massacred by one of their own—the heir to the throne, Prince Dipendra.

The bizarre episode of regicide plunged the country into the world's spotlight.

Prince Dipendra, purportedly crazed with anger that his family were not allowing him to marry the woman he loved, and fuelled by a cocktail of drugs and alcohol, walked into the dining room and slaughtered most of his family with a machine gun. He shot his father first, then turned his rage on eight other members of his immediate family, including his mother, Queen Aishwarya, his brother Prince Nirajan, and his sister Princess Shruti. After trying to blow his own brains out, Prince Dipendra died two days later in hospital.

It was the worst mass killing of royalty since the Romanovs were murdered in 1918 during the Russian civil war. Ruit received a phone call in the middle of the night at his apartment telling him the news that 'His Majesty has just been shot'. 'We were just in disbelief. Nanda and I simply could not believe it at first. We thought it was some joker, playing a hoax,' he recalls.

'We were all absolutely devastated,' Ruit says. 'I had such an affinity with him. He was such a good man, a man of the people. We were on very good terms and I had seen him the week before for his glaucoma. I loved his simplicity, his love of the people. He had shared his many thoughts with me. He really wanted the Maoists to sit down with him and work it out, for the good of the country.'

After the initial physical shock, and what seemed like the arrival of every media organisation in the world to cover the tragedy in Kathmandu, the entire nation went into mourning. There was a huge outpouring of grief when the king's body was taken to the funeral pyres of the Pashupatinath temple by the Bagmati River. Thousands crammed onto the streets to wail and say farewell.

Ruit, Nanda and the children gathered on the roof of a building near the palace to watch the procession.

Ruit's voice quavers as he recalls that grim day when many Nepalese felt as if they had lost a father. The entire city closed down. All the shops rolled their shutters down, and the restaurants locked their doors. The streets were filled with people crying, and beating their chests. As the funeral procession passed by, thousands threw flowers and white scarves at the coffins. It was a genuine outpouring of grief and sorrow, the likes of which Nepal had never seen before.

'All we could think of was what we had lost. I was inconsolably sad. I felt that we had lost someone who was so great for our country. I think a lot of people still miss him. A lot of people feel their guardian had gone,' he says. Like most men, Ruit shaved his head out of respect and grief. It was the end of the royal family which had occupied the throne in Nepal for more than 200 years.

'And as we predicted and expected, his death was the start of a series of tragedies for our country. We've never really recovered. The downfall of Nepali history really came from the royal massacre.'

22

ON A CLEAR DAY

Despite decades of extraordinary results, providing thousands of people with a new life, Ruit's surgical technique continued to be viewed by some in the international ophthalmic community with derision or disdain. It was regarded as a cheaper, second-rate way of restoring sight to the poorest people on the planet.

But international opinion about him finally began to shift after a dramatic head-to-head contest with one of America's top cataract surgeons. Ruit's work was finally given the global gold stamp of approval in 2005 when Dr David F Chang was invited to take part in a clinical trial with Ruit at the Pullahari monastery about 40 minutes north of Kathmandu.

Chang had to work so hard to keep up with Ruit that he likened the day to 'being a contestant on *Iron Chef*'. In a makeshift operating room in a Buddhist schoolroom, Chang buckled down to work with his usual finesse, tackling more than 50 patients blinded by mature cataracts. He had brought along his $100,000 state-of-the-art phacoemulsification machine from

California, which, with its ultrasonic probe, is the most sophisticated way of removing cataracts in the developed world.

In his temporary operating theatre next door, Ruit quietly worked through a similar-sized case load. The barefoot surgeon performed his operations using his simple toolkit of scissors, knives, forceps and cannula probe. Aside from his steriliser and $9000 microscope, none of Ruit's instruments required electricity.

Despite the breathtaking surroundings—the monastery, which is studded with hundreds of exotic subtropical trees and flowers, and which seems to float like a heavenly realm above the chaos of Kathmandu—Chang found himself pushed to the very limits of his abilities during the one-and-a-half-day trial.

His theatre door kept swinging open, and, one after the other, a conveyor belt of challenging cases was brought to his operating table. Almost every one of the patients had the massive calcified advanced cataracts Chang usually saw only a few times each year at his California clinic. Extracting them using phacoemulsification was unrelenting work.

'It was an incredibly stressful two days,' he admits. 'It's never good for your reputation to operate in a strange place, in the developing world after a long plane flight, but 80 per cent of the cases were the sort of exceptionally difficult cases that I'd only occasionally see at home. I really had to work hard just to complete my share of the patients and to keep up with Ruit. I was completely spent by the end of the day.'

The results of the clinical trial were patently clear. Despite the simplicity of his equipment and costing about an eighth of the price, Ruit's patients could see just as well as Chang's the next day. A year later, Ruit's patients were measured again. Their vision was still of equal quality to those Chang had operated on.

In fact, Ruit's technique was not only faster and cheaper, it was also more appropriate for advanced cases. Chang openly admits he uses Ruit's technique on the very worst cases and the densest cataracts he sees in his Californian clinic.

It had been a long time coming, but the trial finally gave Ruit the international reputation he deserved.

'Doctors like Ruit have a lot to teach us in the developed world,' he says. 'Watching him at work, and his high-volume, low-cost cataract surgery, was nothing short of a marvel.'

Ruit says that one day something far less invasive will probably be used to treat cataracts, such as medical drops that dissolve the clouded areas. It might be a robot that does the surgeries on a conveyor belt. Surgery will be so fast and straightforward, like 'getting your coat dry-cleaned', as he puts it.

But in the meantime, there is still so much work to do. Ruit wants to leave a legacy not just in bricks and mortar, through his community hospitals, but by training an army of eye doctors; he loves fostering the careers of younger surgeons who are spreading his technique like wildfire throughout the developing world.

Ruit's favourite way of training is to have two or three surgeons working alongside him in his operating theatre. This way, the most delicate of manoeuvres are magnified on a television-sized screen inside the theatre, which the surgeons watch with hawk-like intensity.

Ruit teaches according to their level. With someone from Indonesia who has had fewer advantages and is low in confidence, Ruit will be gentle and encouraging. But with graduates from elite Western ophthalmology colleges, he will be a hard taskmaster. As Tabin puts it: 'He's an expert in getting surgeons from good to great. He expects perfection.'

It is not just doctors who are being trained in the Nepalese art of eye surgery. Entire medical teams—nurses, anaesthetists, technicians and clinic managers—fly in from every corner of the world for expert tuition at Tilganga. They fly in from India, Pakistan, Bhutan, Myanmar, Indonesia, North Korea, China, Thailand, Cambodia, Vietnam, the Maldives, Ethiopia, Mongolia, Kazakhstan, Ghana, Uganda, Sudan, Iraq, South America and South Africa. They stay for weeks at the hospital, absorbing the system Ruit and Tilganga have elevated to an art form in order to replicate it when they return home.

Often the real training begins when the teams are dispatched to an eye camp in a small village in the hills or mountains. Here, Ruit's elegant, but precise system, which one volunteer described as 'like the inner workings of a Swiss watch', is drummed into them. Everything has to be planned to perfection. Can the patients walk into the eye camp, from along rocky mountain trails? Can 500 patients be easily fed? Can they be housed in tents or makeshift accommodation while they recover? Can everyone be screened in an efficient way? Will everyone receive proper counselling, so they understand what's going to happen afterwards and that they need to come back for check-ups?

Job Heintz says that part of the magic of Tilganga's training system is that it creates 'a sense of the possible'.

'If you took these teams to America or the UK or Australia, they may not believe they could do the same thing when they got back home. But seeing that Ruit does it, in one of the poorest countries in the world, creates this incredible sense of possibility for them. They go home believing and knowing they can do the same thing,' Heintz says.

One of the most important things the team learns is how to be self-sustaining. It's something that's absolutely crucial in countries where the government is unable or unwilling to pay for health care, and foreign aid is patchy. If they can't sustain themselves, they won't survive. The key is replicating Ruit's sliding scale of payment for the operations, a brilliant idea born out of sheer necessity.

'We started trying out the sliding scale at Tilganga, mainly because we had no other option,' Ruit says. 'We had no other resources. There were no grants. It was the only way we could afford to buy beds, and pay the staff. It was the only way we could make the hospital self-sustaining.

'Because of the credibility of my work, we knew we could invite powerful people to come and have surgery. The results are always good and they are happy to pay the full price. Then out of that money, we are able to provide for a large number of people who cannot pay to have free surgery. The poor receive exactly the same quality surgery, but they pay less. So, there is no such thing as second-class sight. Everyone gets first-class sight, no matter how rich or poor they are.'

As he enters his sixth decade, Ruit's hands are rock steady. But he is also increasingly aware of his personal limitations. He's more reflective than ever before, as well as frank about his faults and flaws.

One of these moments was realising that he needed to step away from the governance of the hospital.

Tilganga had become so much bigger than he ever imagined, with more than 400 employees and a complex hierarchy. He began accepting the fact that colleagues such as Dr Reeta Gurung were much better at running the hospital than he was. And that there was a need for more managers—corporate managers—as well as financial and governance experts.

'Everyone is born with strengths and weaknesses; my strength has always been in my hands and my eyes. I took far too long to appoint Reeta as the CEO. I lack the culture of corporate management. I'm good with managing my immediate team but not large-scale corporate management. I'm a bit slack when it comes to being decisive. I'm full of faults, you see. What I've learned is that it is better to stick to what you're good at. That's what I feel more and more. Nowadays, I've started saying, "That's not for me. Somebody else should do this." It's become very clear that the right way for me to spend my days is to sit at the operating table, helping people see. I want to keep doing this for as long as I can.'

It was a relief to step away from the administration, and concentrate on his patients—as well as training his latest 'batch', as he calls them, of up-and-coming surgeons. One of the major things he drums into them, as well as technical finesse, is that a little kindness goes a long way.

No matter how many patients he has operated on, Ruit still likes to connect with each and every one. Even if it's just for a few moments. He might reach out and put his hand on their shoulder and explain what he's going to do. 'It's an exchange of positive energy. If you do this, then the sincerity of what you do will bear fruit in the long term. You gain an excellent reputation, which is more valuable than money.'

He teaches the young surgeons to think of the patient lying in front of them as someone from their family. It might be their mother. Their father. Their brother. Their sister. You never know, it might be a boy from Walung, all alone in a strange hospital.

It might even be a Maoist rebel, brandishing a machine gun. Because the harsh reality of staging eye camps throughout every region of Nepal meant that for many years, his surgical team often had to run the gauntlet of explosives, Molotov cocktails, machine guns and hand grenades.

Nepal is thought of as a country of peaceful Sherpa guides and tinkling temple bells, but during the Nepalese Civil War, the country was torn by bloody domestic strife.

More than one million Nepalese peasants are estimated to have been recruited as Maoist soldiers, in an attempt to overcome centuries of suppression, and to overthrow a succession of corrupt governments after the country voted to become a constitutional monarchy in 1990. The aim of their brutal uprising was straightforward—they wanted to alleviate poverty.

By the late 1990s, when the rebels controlled more than a third of the country, being pulled over at their checkpoints became as commonplace for Ruit and his mobile clinics as stopping to re-fuel for petrol. But after the windows had been wound down and the rebels discovered it was Ruit sitting resolutely in the passenger seat, the soldiers would usually wave him through with their Kalashnikovs and a nod, or a friendly smile.

The rebels respected the doctor's work restoring sight to the poorest peasants no matter what caste or creed. Clad in their military uniform and a cap with a star on it, they called him 'Dr Sahib', meaning 'respected doctor', and offered cups of tea and biscuits. Several times they even let Ruit and his team use their headquarters—usually a former army post or police station—as makeshift field hospitals.

Some politicians felt Ruit should have turned his back on the Maoists, and refused to treat them. He certainly disagreed with their violent methods. He abhorred the slogan they'd borrowed from the Chinese communist leader, Mao Tse-Tung: 'Political power grows out of the barrel of a gun.'

But he was sympathetic to their cause and worked out a way to discreetly treat any Maoist soldier who came to Tilganga or any of the eye camps.

Mostly they got in touch with Khim Gurung, one of Ruit's assistants who organised the camps, but they also approached Ruit personally many times, too, and each time, he was more than happy to talk to them.

Ruit built up a good rapport with many of the leaders, who respected his work. They'd meet out in the field, while he was setting up a camp, and he would always tell them the same thing: they had to lay down their weapons and become a political party. He told them they had to try talking to the government, and that he was always happy to act as a go-between.

'It was the only way they could change things for the better. The violence sickened me, and I knew it wouldn't achieve anything. But I continued treating them, no matter what people said. I thought it was vital that we kept operating in Maoist strongholds because they were usually hubs of blind-ness. I thought it was important to show that Tilganga was beyond politics. And, besides, they were often young men with simple weapons, who, out of desperation, were trying to make a better life for themselves and their families.'

Every evening, at about 5 or 6 p.m., whatever region he was in, after Ruit had finished working on his last patient for the day, a girl from the Maoist rebels would come and sit quietly in the waiting room. The girl would always be wearing a pink kurta—a long loose tunic and trousers in the style of cotton pyjamas—which were the secret signal to Ruit that a Maoist soldier needed treatment.

'Sometimes it was almost as if I could feel their pain as they lay in front of me on the operating table,' Ruit says. 'Many of them felt truly exploited, unable to gain an education, or buy land. They were people like you and me who just wanted the same as everyone else in the world—schools, hospitals, jobs, the end of the caste system. They wanted the chance to give their children a better future than their own.'

The plight of the women soldiers who donned a military uniform and picked up firearms always made Ruit's heart sink. One came to him for treatment at an outreach camp and told him she lived in a house with electricity. Although she'd had no schooling herself, she dreamed of sending her own two children to school, but their chances were slight. Their future, as far as she could see it, was to resign themselves to continue to eke out an existence on the family's small farm. 'The final straw came when she'd borrowed money to take her sick mother to the nearest clinic, only to have the money lender threaten to take away her goats and chickens when she was unable to repay him on time,' he says.

As Ruit operated on her, all he could think of was that she could have been him, if his father hadn't sent him to India to gain a proper education at a boarding school. His background gave him great sympathy for the Maoists he treated. 'They were just so downtrodden. All they really wanted was the chance of a better life.'

His heart went out to them, but he and his team were always on edge as they approached one of the Maoist-held zones. It was hard not to feel alarmed; the buildings were emblazoned in red paint with symbols of hammers and sickles, or painted with fierce communist slogans such as 'Burn the Old House Down'. It was intimidating. There was always the sense that things could turn nasty if they were in the wrong place at the wrong time. They were working in areas, after all, in which the police themselves were often afraid to enter.

A few times they came far too close to the fighting for comfort. Once in south-west Nepal, Ruit was halfway through a cataract operation at an eye camp, making a delicate incision into the patient's cornea, when the building was rocked by a deafening explosion as the rebels blew up a local police station. A long blast of machine gun fire then shattered the peace of the countryside around them.

Ruit, shaken, kept his hand rock-steady on his scalpel, reassuring the patient lying on the table in front of him that the rebels were too far away to cause any problems, and calmly finished extracting the patient's cataracts. He's a man of great forbearance, but this particular episode enraged him. He was furious with the rebels for putting his team and his patients in danger. And he burned with rage at the police for the way they retaliated by coming down on the rebels so violently.

'A lot of the peasants waiting to have their operations were very worried, especially the poor man lying on the table in front of me, but we told them they would be okay, and carried on our work,' Ruit recalls. The local police eventually escorted Ruit and his team from the building back to their lodgings at the end of their day's work.

In his small hostel room that night, Ruit's mind turned instinctively toward home. His private practice had finally grown enough for the children to attend the best private schools in Kathmandu. When Sagar was seven, they had enrolled him at St Xavier's Godavari School, a Jesuit boarding school about an hour and a half out of Kathmandu. He was still his mother's favourite, and Nanda would count the hours until he'd come home again, on the weekends and during the holidays. Meanwhile, every morning, Serabla and Satenla headed off on the bus to a strict, all-girls' convent school, St Mary's High School.

Both Sagar and Serabla were turning out well. They were typical of eldest children—reserved and responsible—whereas Satenla, the youngest, was more pampered. 'She got away with a lot more,' Serabla says. 'She used to fight with Dad and cry.'

He always missed them when he was away, especially the girls' and Nanda's chatter over dinner at night. His favourite part of the day was after dinner, hearing about their day at school, and giving his girls a big pat on the head when they did well in their exams or essays.

He and Nanda were proud of their strong work ethic, and especially that they had no airs and graces. Just as important as sending them to the best schools they could afford was endowing them with a sense of being loved. 'I think they can see our love for them is sincere and unconditional. And that we have always set very high moral values for them.'

Having had such an authoritarian father, Ruit hopes he was a lot softer with his own children. 'You'll have to ask them about it, but I don't think they'd be as frightened of me as I was of my dad when I was a boy. It was always very hard to talk to Dad, he was hard to communicate with, it was hard to be close to him. I hope my children don't feel the same way about me. I hope I'm a lot easier to talk to.'

Ruit is, at heart, like so many Nepalese, a family man. Every two weeks, the Ruit clan would gather together for a 'pot luck' lunch on the weekend, when everyone would bring a dish of food. They would often gather at Tenzin Ukyab's home and sit around together all day, the older ones playing cards, the younger ones playing games on the lawn.

Much of Ruit's motivation, going to such lengths to restore sight in far-flung rural villages, and venturing into such dangerous zones, is the desire to give his patients a second chance at the same simple pleasures and a good home life that he revels in.

'Restoring the natural rhythm of family life, restoring the balance of the communities, that's what it's all about, what I hope my work is doing,' he says.

It appalled Ruit that money lenders were still rife in many of the villages they visited. He views it as one of the most notorious practices in rural areas. That, along with the medieval practice of bonded labour, which sometimes resulted in a whole family being indentured to an unscrupulous landlord, working without payment on his farm until they had paid their debts. Even worse, sometimes a daughter was sent into bonded labour, a euphemism for prostitution, in the larger towns such as Pokhara. It was exploitation of the cruellest kind, and there had been absolutely nothing the Nepalese could do about it. 'It's a lot better now, but for a long time it was a feudal society where the innocent were quite badly exploited.'

What saddens Ruit is that while the Maoist movement did create some awareness about the vast inequity between the haves and the have-nots, the violence and destruction only led to Nepal floundering economically. It remains one of the world's poorest countries, with 80 per cent of the population living below the poverty line.

'The timing was terrible. At the same time as our rivals, India and China, were forging ahead, and really starting to prosper, Nepal ended up going backwards. We lost so much foreign investment because of the instability the Maoists caused. Looking back, the ten-year struggle didn't achieve anything.'

Matthieu Ricard, the Buddhist monk and author of the book *Happiness*, and a fan of Ruit's, says the fact that the Maoist rebels allowed Ruit to work in their strongholds showed how highly esteemed he had become.

'The Maoists were very formidable, very tough on everyone, and very protective of their turf. There were a lot of charities they didn't let in at all, even those doing necessary things such as building wells. But when it came to Ruit, they just waved him through. They saw that his only motivation was to help people. He was a cultural hero to them.'

Without realising it, Ruit has inspired countless young people to have the courage of their convictions. The fact that a boy from the border of Tibet could go on to spearhead a world revolution in wiping out blindness has prompted many students in Nepal, India and Bhutan to enrol in medicine or go to university—even if nobody in their family had done so before.

One of the surgeons who works alongside him in Bhutan, Dr Dechen Wangmo, says Ruit has inspired a whole generation of young people in the Dragon Kingdom to become doctors—including her own daughter.

'His sort of talent is so rare. He's so physically heavy but his hands are so delicate. There are no wasteful movements. Everyone can learn to play the piano but only a few are as truly gifted as he is. I remember the first camp we went to, we did about 700 cataracts in five days. It was absolutely incredible. And yet he made it look so easy. Only great surgeons do that. Usually surgeons with great talent like him emigrate to the US or the UK, but he's stayed here in the Himalayas to make a difference.'

Young doctors starting out at the hospital often ask Ruit for advice. What he tells them is that there are no shortcuts. 'You have to be committed. Work out what you are really good at and capitalise on your strengths. Then work really hard. If you can find work you love, then do it. Work with passion, with your heart, as if every person you meet is the most important person you meet that day. It makes a huge difference. Every kind of job has meaning if you have the right motivation,' he tells them.

What about people stuck in a dead-end office job where they spend much of the day staring out the window? If you are the breadwinner, and you need to feed your family, you need to be practical, he says. Your family is your first priority. But it's also important to have a vision, too. 'Everyone has the right to dream,' he says. 'If it means you get up early, before your family wakes up, or stay up late at night, to study, and move into a job that you're passionate about, then you should definitely do that.'

Good management skills are drummed into the teams that come to Tilganga. They learn how to communicate with staff, how to inspire them, and how to set a good example. His own team members are living proof that his approach works. Many have been with him for more than 30 years; they look like they'd run through fire for him. So what is his secret?

'I see the best in others. I watch what people are good at and then set them doing it. I harness their particular talents. Everyone has strengths and weaknesses; being a good manager means recognising and drawing on their strengths. It's also important to create a good atmosphere in your team. To really care for each other. I try to really look after my staff. I make sure they are all happy and well. I give them opportunities, such as sending them to the US or Australia or the UK to enhance their skills by learning with great surgeons. And I share my vision with them, so they know they are part of something greater than themselves.'

'He can be a hard taskmaster but there's no doubt he brings out the best in people and inspires great loyalty,' Tabin says. 'He inspires through his charisma. His immediate team have been with him for decades and he has elevated them through the system. To work at Tilganga is a really prestigious position in Kathmandu. He's created something everyone has pride in. It's not a job. He's created a mission people approach with joy. Everyone in Nepal knows Tilganga. It's become a household name because it is something they are so proud of.'

Matthieu Ricard often cites Ruit's approach when asked about successful leadership.

'I realised I kept on bringing patients to him for treatment just for the joy of seeing him and the way he treats them, and his team. Some organisations just work really well—the people there are efficient, good, and reliable and dedicated, but when you have hundreds working for him, as Ruit does, and it still works brilliantly, it takes a special quality. It works because the leader himself is a great source of inspiration, in terms of integrity, in terms of what he is achieving. What Ruit shows his team is that it is not how much money the organisation made in the year, but how much suffering they alleviated during the year. When you go to Tilganga, or to one of their camps, immediately everybody is kind, efficient, and takes care of you. They find your files and go out of their way to help you if you need help getting home. They all seem to be infused with the same kind of willingness to serve. That really comes from his inspiration, and not in an ordinary way but the sheer strength of what he is.'

Tilganga doctors have even started training days for traditional healers from rural areas. These are the local village men—some might derisively describe them as witch doctors—who may unintentionally make matters worse by telling patients that their blindness is a curse, bestowed from a past bad deed. They might suggest superstitious remedies such as killing goats or chicken, or even trying homemade potions. Ruit, as diplomatic as ever, puts it this way: 'What we have learnt is that we can't change the healers' livelihoods, but we can teach them how not to harm their community. We encourage them to send the blind to Tilganga or one of our clinics or camps, so they are in expert hands.'

Of course, surgical mistakes still happen. He estimates 1 per cent of cases need to be corrected the next day. 'I've had cases where the patient had to be re-stitched and blood had to be washed away after surgery the next day. That happens. Sometimes the intraocular lens is not positioned properly. You have to insert it again a few days later.'

Ruit is devastated every time he comes across people who have incurable blindness in remote areas and has to tell the patient there is nothing that can be done. 'The worst is telling parents nothing can be done for a blind child because they have left it too long before they tried to get help. There is nothing worse than that. Nothing worse. It spurs me on to work even harder that day to give sight to everyone else that I possibly can,' he says.

The most infuriating are families who keep their older blind relatives in a back room for so long that their blindness becomes incurable. They simply don't care for them enough to bring them to a hospital or clinic. 'These poor souls are treated worse than animals,' Ruit says. 'At least animals are led outside and in the sunshine, and are given enough food.' These are the forgotten ones that are beyond help, who have been left in a pitiful state; they are alone, dejected, depressed, malnourished, sometimes half-deranged. Having to tell them and their families that it is too late to cure them, that nothing can be done, he says, is the 'very worst feeling in the world'. He always insists they bring them out from the back room, include them in family life, and give them all the medicine and good food they can.

23

PRIVATE HEARTACHE

By the mid 2000s, Ruit's career had suddenly taken off to an entirely new level. He was earning a reputation as one of the world's finest surgeons and humanitarians, and was showered in prestigious awards. In 2006, he won the Philippines' Ramon Magsaysay Award, which many consider as the Asian equivalent of the Nobel Prize. The next year he was awarded both Thailand's Prince Mahidol Award and the *Reader's Digest* Asian of the Year award. He was asked to make speeches and give media interviews. Long photographic features on his work ran in *TIME* magazine and the *South China Morning Post*. American broadcaster Lisa Ling's documentaries on his work in Nepal and North Korea for *National Geographic* brought his work into the limelight in the United States.

As his cousin Tenzing Ukyab puts it: 'There was a time when I used to take him a present every time he got an award. Then it became too many and too often, and I couldn't keep up. Many of them I didn't even hear about because he would be the last person to mention it.'

Ruit used his growing reputation to continue spreading his technique to the world's blindness trouble spots. In 2005, he felt confident enough to venture into a part of the world no-one would ever have dreamed possible: 'The Hermit Kingdom' of North Korea.

Ruit's life had been in danger during Nepal's bloody domestic war, but the most frightened he ever felt was undoubtedly the fortnight he and his team spent at an eye camp in the Democratic People's Republic of Korea (DPRK).

How on earth did a Nepalese doctor end up performing his medical miracles in one of the most forbidding countries in the world? The opportunity arose to work in North Korea, with its notorious human rights violations, and equally notorious nuclear weapons program, when a patient he'd just seen in his private clinic in Kathmandu, Mr Kim, handed him a card that read, 'Consul of DPRK'.

Ruit has never professed to be a human rights activist. The higher the rate of blindness, the keener he is to help, no matter what the country's political ideology or religion might be. He simply draws a line at war zones. One place he'd like to work in, for instance, is Yemen, one of the Arab world's poorest countries. 'It's a small country and they really need help. But when bombs are falling and guns are shooting in a country, cataracts are not usually a priority. That's one place we can't go to.'

All he knew was that North Korea was one of the world's worst trouble spots of blindness; it was a powerful pull. More than half a million people are estimated to be blind there, a rate about ten times higher than in the West. Ruit knew they would have had very little access to doctors. And that a good proportion of them would have been blind in both eyes for years.

He immediately tried to build a rapport with the quietly spoken consul.

He invited Mr Kim to visit Tilganga the next day. He showed him the gleaming equipment, training centre and the hundreds of patients treated every day. His eyes boggled, Ruit says, presumably as he realised how much Tilganga could help the blind in his country.

Over dinner a few nights later, Ruit suggested to Mr Kim that he hold a surgical workshop in the DPRK. If it worked, he would train as many doctors and nurses as he could, so they could stand on their own two feet, rather than relying on help from foreigners.

It took years of negotiations, as hatred of foreigners and outside help, including humanitarian missions, was still strong. But finally, in 2005, Ruit and his small team flew into the capital, Pyongyang.

From the air, it looked like they were entering a communist country during the Cold War era in the 1950s. Interspersing square, grim-looking concrete buildings were wide concrete highways, which were almost completely empty as cars were a luxury only for the elite.

Accompanying Ruit was Reeta Gurung, photographer Michael Amendolia, and a small team led by his stalwart camp coordinator Khim Gurung, known affectionately as 'camp commandant'.

As soon as they landed in Pyongyang, their personal freedom was curtailed. All phones, cameras and passports were confiscated. Two guards accompanied them the entire trip, watching their every move and listening to everything they said. There was not one moment when they could wander off and walk around unobserved. There was no outside influence at all. Access to the internet, radio, books or magazines was forbidden. They were completely cut off from the world.

The American journalist Lisa Ling, who in 2006 accompanied Ruit into North Korea for the documentary television channel *National Geographic*, remembers how unnerving it was to be so cut off from the world.

'I was quite shocked by the protocols we had to adhere to just to get in,' she says. 'We had to meet with the North Korean ambassador to Nepal before we'd even got on the plane. There were all these formalities. I was really surprised they didn't do any kind of Google search on me, because I was already on a national daytime talk show in the US. I was probably a little naïve when I went in under the auspices of the medical team because my understanding at that time was that if they found out I was a journalist, then I would simply be ejected out of the country, or expelled. But as I found out later when my sister was detained, it could have been far worse. (In 2009, Lisa's sister Laura, also a journalist, was detained by North Korean border guards and sentenced to twelve years' hard labour for not having a visa. Kim Jong-Il pardoned her and her group of colleagues the day before American president Bill Clinton arrived to lobby for their release.)

'When we landed, they took our passports and our technological devices and they had about eight escorts monitoring us all the time. They even stayed in our guesthouse. I was permitted to go for a jog but I always had a couple of eyes watching me as I jogged laps around the building. It really was a surreal experience because growing up in America I had no experience of communism. I remember I brought a fashion magazine in my bag with me, and the young man minding me scolded me. He said it would give people wrong ideas. I remember feeling very isolated. I felt if anything happened to me, no-one would know and there would be this inability to communicate with my loved ones. I didn't think about the fact that I could possibly be arrested and detained for a lengthy period of time.'

Officials picked them up in an old Mercedes Benz car. As they swept through the capital, the only decorations they could see were brightly lit monuments glorifying 'Dear Leader, Kim Jong Il'. There were no billboards or neon signs. Everyone was in drab-coloured clothes. At night, the city was dark as the power was cut off. It was eerily quiet.

They travelled to the port city of Haeju, about 100 kilometres south of the capital, the next day, sobered by the scenes from the train windows of lean-looking labourers doing manual work on the farms. 'I'm used to seeing poverty, so it wasn't really a shock to me,' says Ruit. 'I've seen a lot of that in Nepal as well as many places in Africa and Asia.'

But what he was shocked by was the severity of the cataracts in the 1000 blind people awaiting him at a large, Soviet-style hospital. The examination room was crammed with farmers, peasants, children and the elderly. All of them had been hand-picked by the government and, as Ruit had rightly guessed, all of them had been completely blind for years.

Over the years, Ruit has built up a lot of stamina; he can easily operate all day, seeing an average of 70 patients. But that bitterly cold surgery—it was on average minus

10 degrees—working with the barest, most basic of equipment, much of which his team had brought themselves from Kathmandu, was a true test of his endurance.

He had a jacket and some sweaters, but it was still so cold that he had to operate with a couple of blankets wrapped around him. He kept his hands warm by constantly rubbing them. There was no light and no electricity, forcing Ruit to send Khim Gurung back to Pyongyang for a generator. The government provided Khim with one, as well as car to take it back to Haeju.

Most of the patients had never seen a doctor before. Many of them were very fearful and Ruit tried to speak to them as soothingly as he could through the interpreter.

Over the next eleven days, Ruit and his team screened 2230 patients who had been hand-chosen by government officials, and restored sight to 702 people.

'It was a very bleak scene. My heart went out to so many of them. I'd never seen so many advanced cases. Everyone of them had been blind in both eyes for years. Almost all of them had totally white cataracts. Once I saw the magnitude of the problem, I was so glad we'd decided to come, despite all our fear of being deported, or worse, thrown into prisons.'

Reeta Gurung has been back to North Korea several times since that first trip to train more than 40 surgeons. 'The atmosphere was like a big thick cloud covering you,' she recalls. 'You don't have the freedom to do anything. It's when you go to a place like that and come back home that you realise what freedom really means. You really feel the tension. Everything is very tightly controlled. I remember getting a sense of how desperate the patients were when I peeked into the lunch room [of the hospital] one day. I saw a mother and an older person, maybe her dad, sitting on the floor, desperately clutching the papers for them to receive an examination. I saw then for the first time how much they needed medical help.'

Ruit and his team were used to seeing all sorts of reactions when patients can finally see again, but the scenes that they witnessed in North Korea astonished them. The patients didn't smile or laugh, or thank Ruit or the team. Instead, most of them rushed to express their adoration to the Dear Leader, bowing and crying in gratitude in front of giant portraits of Kim Jong-Il. 'We praise you!' they said, with tears running down their cheeks.

They were convinced it was their supreme leader who had restored their sight rather than modern surgical skills. 'Some people might call it an extreme personality cult, but I had no problem with their devotion to their leader,' Ruit said. 'I didn't want any thanks. I did my job well, and the elation on their faces spoke a thousand words.

'I wasn't really affected by them prostrating to their leader like that—they believe he is next to God. If it were a Muslim country, they would talk to Allah, and if it were a Christian country, they would talk to Jesus and Mary. If it is a Hindu country, they would talk to Lord Krishna or Shiva. We weren't there to change the political system, after all, we were there to help them see again.

'People are the same wherever you go. They have two eyes, two hands, and all the same desires as everyone else. They were just a lot of people who needed our love. They are the same as you or me. The two North Korean doctors watching over us were totally amazed by the results. We had a meeting with the minister of health later that day, who said, 'We want to make this an ongoing program.' I don't think I've ever felt so proud in my life.'

Since that first camp, Tilganga has held more than ten surgical camps in North Korea, trained more than 40 doctors and nurses, and performed operations on more than 7000 patients. 'What I'm proud of is that we have helped them believe in their own merits, that they can do it as well as anywhere else in the world.'

On the first trip to Haeju in 2005, the most terrifying moment came on the train trip back to Pyongyang. A guard started opening up their luggage and rummaging, excruciatingly slowly, through everyone's belongings. Amendolia had taken about 25 reels of photographs. He had been approved as a member of the medical team, but he didn't have permission to be there as a journalist—let alone to take film out of the country—so they had divided it up among everyone's luggage.

Ruit was trying hard not to look nervous, but the sweat was trickling down the back of his hair into his collar. His heart was pounding. He knew this was a country capable of sending entire families and their children to notorious work camps for the rest of their lives for minor transgressions, such as saying anything critical of the Dear Leader. And here they were with bags packed with hundreds of illegal photographs. Ruit thought they were going to be arrested, thrown in jail or deported. After what seemed like an eternity, the guard moved onto another group, but everyone—Ruit and Amendolia especially—felt as if they'd lost a few years of their lives.

~

Despite all his success, there was one thing Ruit continued to dread: live surgery. The largest crowd he performed in front of was a gathering of 4000 public health professionals in the Philippines. In Hong Kong, Thailand and China, he would submit to the public ordeal, as he simultaneously explained his every move to audiences of more than 500 as they watched his every microscopic move on a giant screen.

He's one of the few surgeons in the world who can carry it off with aplomb, but even he finds it an ordeal.

'Live surgery is still very, very daunting for me,' he says. 'Nerve-wracking. You have to mentally prepare the night before, rehearsing every move in your mind. And try to get a really good night's sleep. Then you need complete composure as you do it.'

But the gruelling process is also what he calls his 'greatest public relations weapon'.

The public ordeal had a knack of paying off every time. 'Seeing my work so clearly always seems to encourage generous people give something to Tilganga,' he says. Witnessing his work has the same impact on smaller groups, too; a Nepalese entrepreneur whose family were invited into his surgery to watch him at work afterwards donated half a million rupees toward his cause.

It doesn't take long for most observers to tap into the magic of Ruit's work. The operating chair is the most comfortable place in the world for Ruit, and watching him at work is just as comforting.

The pre-theatre atmosphere is similar to that of an orchestra about to go out and perform. There's the ebb and flow of gentle teasing and shared jokes, the easy camaraderie of a team who have worked together for decades and who can anticipate each other's every move.

A hush descends at the start of the day's work as the door swings open and the first patient is led inside.

The team moves into action, unwrapping the plastic around new disposable instruments, adjusting the reassuring beeping of the phacoemulsification machine as Ruit bends over his patients with his Muller Corella microscope, the Rolls Royce of microscopes, which shows his every move on a television screen in the theatre for trainee surgeons to watch. He is always barefoot, his wide sole on the floor pedal delicately focusing the microscope.

Often, once the patients are helped off the operating table and led toward the doors, they will turn and clasp their hands in gratitude, bowing to him. It's one of the few times that Ruit, who steadfastly keeps his cool when anyone praises him, seems genuinely pleased.

One of the most difficult patients he's ever operated on was a mentally unstable man in China with an extremely mature cataract. Ruit was making the initial entry into the eye with his knife when the patient rose up from the table and began staggering around the room with the instruments still sticking into his eyeball, like something out of a horror movie.

'You can't physically force people, and we couldn't speak to him as he had no English or Nepali. It was a difficult moment,' Ruit recalls. Eventually, they found a nurse who spoke Chinese and asked her to come in. She came running into the theatre and spoke to him very quietly; in the end, it was physical touch that helped—the loving touch of the nurse who gently stroked his cheek, and spoke to him quietly, holding his hand. Slowly, she got the patient back down on the table. As Ruit was approaching the sensitive part once the cataract was out, and was sealing the wound, the nurses held him very firmly until they had finished the procedure.

'We can communicate a lot without words. We never, ever, try to do anything with force. If you do it by force then the patients will rebound by force. If you try to caress them with a kind touch they always understand, I think. If someone with soft gentle hands touches the cheeks and gives them a little massage on the hand, they feel very comforted. If someone is really caring, perhaps holding their hand and caressing them, then that's very good.'

Ruit swells with pride whenever he talks about his team. 'I always say I have the blessing of a wonderful team. They are so efficient and I don't have to say anything. Everything gets done and not many people are lucky like that. I know they have unquestionable faith in what I am doing, but, for my part, I have tried to share my vision with them. I'd like to do more of that. Some of them have been with me for more than 30 years. The staff completely spoil me—some of my friends from the West really envy me. It's taken a long time, but I feel that the team has been defined and sharpened so well that they are one of the best teams in the world. We spend the whole day together in Tilganga, and weeks together when we are on the road. We work very hard together getting our equipment on the back of trucks, holding the microscope in our arms and carrying instruments in our bags, and, when we first started, we'd sleep on the top of cow sheds if we had to. We almost always eat together and share drinks in the evening. The camaraderie is fantastic. We always try to create financial incentives, always recognise everyone's efforts, and give them the opportunity for training, and a better workplace. The main thing they all know, I hope, when they're working with me, is that I appreciate them.'

~

Despite Ruit's love of being with his team, sharing his thoughts and dreams with them, there were parts of his life he kept private. What many would have had little idea about, for instance, was that for many years he was in a state of quiet desperation at home, spending hours on the phone and online with an American security network that tracks missing people. He was searching for his brother. After Ladenla had left to study in the United States in 1990, the family had lost contact with him altogether. They were fraught with anxiety about his health.

He traced Ladenla through the Nepalese communities in the United States, and eventually found him repairing the electronics and radio equipment in the boats in the harbour of Bellingham, Washington, just south of the Canadian border. Ruit flew into Seattle Airport and met Dick Litwin, who had driven there from Berkeley to offer his support.

It remains a baffling episode for Litwin. 'Bellingham is a beautiful spot with a small harbour by the ocean. I walked ahead for about twenty minutes while Ruit and Lin [the family's name for Ladenla] stayed 30 paces behind me and spoke softly to each other. Ruit didn't tell me much; like a lot of Asians, he is very private, and if anything negative happens they don't tend to talk about it too much or dwell on it. It was all a bit of a mystery.'

Ruit recalls having a highly emotional lunch with Ladenla that day. 'I cried. Ladenla cried. The person who was looking after him cried. I was so relieved to see my long-lost brother in one piece.'

Eventually, in 2012, Ladenla returned home to Kathmandu, to spend time with his mother Kasang before she succumbed to cancer.

Ruit was initially wary about his brother returning home. He was worried about how this would influence Sagar, Serabla and Satenla, who were all making their way in the world.

Despite his father's urgings not to, Sagar had enrolled in medicine at Manipal College of Medical Sciences in Pokhara, in the foothills of the Himalayas in central Nepal. Serabla had graduated from a business degree at HELP University in Kuala Lumpur, Malaysia. Ruit had first flown with Serabla to Kuala Lumpur to attend her orientation in 2008 and help her settle in. 'He was very emotional saying goodbye to me,' she says. She flew home for the semester breaks, and Skyped home once a week. She had returned to work in Kathmandu in 2013. Satenla, the youngest, was still studying at St Mary's in 2012, and was planning to enrol in Manipal with her brother.

He was hugely protective of them. 'My whole thought is with my children and how I can help them do well.'

But Ruit's fears were assuaged when Sonam bought Ladenla a small house in Kathmandu, and he saw how quietly Ladenla lived, going to the temples and visiting family and friends, focusing on his recovery from his drug addiction.

'He's well now,' says Ruit. 'His English is fantastic, he's

very well presented. He's got wonderful computer skills and some really great, close friends. But I must admit, the whole episode gave me a lot of compassion for anyone and any family with a relative suffering an addiction. It's a terrible thing that causes so much heartache and suffering, not just for the person, but their entire family. I wouldn't wish it upon anybody.'

24

REBUILDING FROM
THE RUINS

It is no stretch of the imagination to see Ruit in another time and place as an army general, rallying the troops. He is at his best in a crisis. On Saturday, 25 April 2015, after a magnitude 7.8 earthquake tore central and eastern Nepal asunder, Ruit, Reeta Gurung and Suhrid Ghimire, the chairman of the Nepal Eye Program, quickly gathered to work out a plan to turn Tilganga into a relief centre.

They decided to keep the hospital open to treat the hundreds of earthquake victims with head, face or eye injuries. But they knew they had to help those most in need—the mountain villagers who had lost everything, and who were stranded in the heavy rains with no food or shelter—as fast as possible. The damage was catastrophic. Many of the villages where families live in mud and thatch houses had been completely levelled.

They swung into action, ordering bulk supplies of instant noodles, rice, dhal, lentils, salt, soap, tarpaulins, water purifying tablets and medicine. Even though it was Sunday, staff came into the courtyard of the hospital voluntarily to pack them and load them onto trucks. The mood was very subdued; more than twenty of the staff had lost their homes, and many had friends or family members who had perished in the disaster.

They hired trucks to drive the supplies as far as they possibly could, up the precipitous roads, toward the villages. Where the roads were impassable or marred by landslides, they coordinated with the Red Cross helicopters who delivered them to the villages. Medical supplies and emergency shelters were also provided.

Ruit made a television appeal, asking for help. He spoke from the heart, saying it would take years for the people of Nepal to rebuild their lives. 'We need to rebuild houses, families, lives and morale,' he said.

Over the years, despite his natural reserve, Ruit had gradually learned the art of public relations.

The support that had been generated by Lisa Ling's documentaries and, in a high-profile column by Nicholas Kristof of the *New York Times* in 2015, as well as a 13-minute segment on *60 Minutes* in the United States in 2016, had made Ruit aware of the power of storytelling. He still feels awkward sitting down in television studios, but knows the value of talking about his work with well-respected journalists. He has had no training in public speaking; he's learnt on the job, a little painfully at times. 'I've learnt to keep it brief and uncomplicated, and just speak from the heart.'

For the earthquake television appeal, he took the same approach.

Within hours, offers of help arrived from every corner of the globe: from the United States, the UK, Australia,

Singapore, Indonesia, Malaysia, Korea, Europe and Switzerland. 'I was absolutely overwhelmed by the response. I thought it would raise a few thousand dollars, but, within a few days, people had pledged almost $1 million. I don't think the people of Nepal realised how fond the rest of the world is of them until then. We were so strengthened by that support. The faith and love we felt from the international community was way beyond my expectations, and I know it kept a lot of people going. The way the Nepalese have dealt with the problem shows just how patient and resilient they are. Despite the magnitude of the damage to their houses and villages; despite all the loss, all the heartache, all the stress, they have remained patient and resilient.'

Ruit was working at his private clinic on that terrifying day. Just before lunchtime, halfway through examining a patient, the patient's chair began to sway toward him. Then he felt *his* chair begin to tilt toward his patients. At first, he thought he'd forgotten his blood pressure medication. It was either that, he thought, or he was dizzy or unwell.

He knew something was wrong when, a few seconds later, the electricity was cut off and the lights went out. All 25 patients were sitting with him in the pitch dark. Then they heard a terrible sound: a deep powerful rumble that sounded like a giant truck heading toward them, or a mountain falling down. As it grew louder and louder, they realised, to their horror, exactly what it was. The shaking lasted for 50 seconds, but for Ruit and everyone trapped inside, it seemed like an eternity. Ruit's clinic was on the ground floor of an older-style building, with only one door out to the street. The ground was lurching and swaying wildly beneath their feet and the contents of the shelves were smashing to the floor all around them. With his heart thudding wildly, and his legs and hands shaking, he calculated that by the time he'd shepherded all 25 patients out into the street, he might not actually make it out himself. 'I remember thinking, *Okay, this is probably it for me, I'm going to die here trapped inside my clinic as the building collapses on top of me. My time has come.*'

Somehow, though, they managed to scramble out into the street, only to meet a scene of chaos, mutilation and gore. The walls of concrete buildings were swaying and crumbling around them, sending clouds of dust high into the air. Wide cracks had opened in the streets. They could hear avalanches from the mountains.

They were all trying to find their feet again, only to be rocked by aftershocks—the first of more than 200 that were to come in the following days. There was no mobile reception and Ruit was beside himself with anxiety about his family on the other side of town.

All he and his patients could do was to hold hands as they looked at the nightmare unfolding around them. The air was filled with the sound of sirens and screaming. People were dying on the side of the road, others were being carried to the hospital on makeshift stretchers. Ruit made his way to the general hospital to help. There were children and babies crying, and people sobbed inconsolably over dead relatives and friends who had been brought in on stretchers. 'There were so many people on stretchers, they were everywhere. Some of them were on intravenous fluid. The most important thing to do at first, was to work out who was dead and who was still alive. The sorrow and panic were hard to describe.'

When the official doctors began racing into the hospital, Ruit began wending his way home through the chaos.

As he raced through the front gate and saw his whole family standing there in the front garden, he crushed them all in a bear hug in relief. He stayed a few hours so that he and Nanda could phone all their relatives and friends to make sure they had survived, and he monitored the news. Soon, word of the death toll started coming through.

Across the country, the losses were immeasurable. As well as killing more than 9000 people and leaving more than half a million Nepalese without homes, it had flattened more than 180 of the city's ancient temples made out of wood and unmortared bricks. These were more than just historical sites; they were ancient, ornate public places where people gathered to socialise and do business.

Such was the earthquake's force that it set off avalanches around Mount Everest, where at least seventeen climbers died. Buildings swayed in Tibet and Bangladesh. Tremors were felt across northern India, killing 34 people and rattling bookcases and light fixtures as far away as New Delhi.

The fact that Tilganga was still standing was a testament to the dedication and hard work of the unofficial building supervisor, Les Douglas. His insistence on building it to Western standards had paid off. With its 4-metre-deep concrete foundation, truckloads of steel, and double-brick cavity walls, it stood unharmed apart from some cracks in the stairwell.

The aftershocks continued and, as night fell, many residents sat on roads afraid to go back indoors. Thousands camped out at the city's parade ground or slept outdoors. Today, many of the hospital staff and family members are still living in tents, with relatives, or in makeshift accommodation. Tilganga, along with many international charities, continues to help build temporary shelters for the worst-hit villages— daunting, grinding work in this already impoverished nation.

Ruit wasn't the only one to spend hours in the middle of the night worrying about what to do if another earthquake hits. For months afterwards, many people suffered a kind of post-traumatic stress disorder, a sense of living constantly on edge, starting at the slightest sound.

The toll on the blind was devastating. Three of Tilganga's thirteen community eye centres which Ruit had first begun in 2000 were flattened and two partly destroyed. More than nine of their regular outreach camps were cancelled, resulting in a backlog of 3000 people.

The first eye camp was held eight months after the earthquake, at Nuwakot, about 75 kilometres north of Kathmandu, where more than 1000 people were killed and 1300 were injured. Despite the fact that winter was setting in, many of them were still living in tents and temporary shelters. It's hard to imagine just how terrifying it must have been for the blind during the earthquake. Imagine feeling the building shudder and shake and start collapsing around you, and not being able to see the door, or being able to race outside and reach open ground. One woman had shouted and cried out to her family all day before she was found trapped under the bed of her collapsed house, covered in bruises and scratches.

The world's media has turned away from the earthquake relief efforts, and, two years later, tourists had only just begun to drift back, slowly resurrecting the central industry on which the nation depends. Meanwhile, after being covered in metal scaffolding for months, the golden spire of Boudhanath Stupa, which collapsed during the earthquake, is back in place. Lit up with fairy lights, reverberating with Tibetan chanting, it draws thousands of locals toward it every morning like a beacon of hope. Not even an earthquake could shake the Nepalese people's deep faith in life.

25

NORTHERN EXPOSURE

The most picturesque places can be deceptive. The former British hill station of Kalimpong, in the Indian state of West Bengal, for instance, might enjoy sweeping panoramas of the Himalayas, but unusually high rates of blindness plague the area.

The Jamgon Kongtrul Memorial Home, like many of the town's church-run schools and private residences, was built during the colonial era on a long ridge overlooking Mount Kanchenjunga, Ruit's home mountain. Since it opened in 2004, more than 20,000 patients have had their eyesight restored there by Ruit and his team.

The Memorial Home, which includes one of Ruit's community clinics, is just one of the 3rd Jamgon Kongtrul's many legacies (he was killed in a car accident in 1992). The idea was born when the lama noticed elderly people doing back-breaking work smashing up rocks on the side of the road. Surely, he could provide them with a roof over their head so they could enjoy the last years of their lives in peace, without worrying about where the next meal was coming from? After nine elderly, destitute people were settled into the colonial-style bungalows that made up his family's former residence, three orphans were also housed there temporarily. Despite fears that they would disrupt the peace and quiet, they proved the opposite, bringing joy to the elderly residents and a family atmosphere to the place. The children unofficially adopt a favourite 'Po Po' (grandfather) or 'Awa' (grandmother).

They clamber onto their laps, wrapping their arms around their necks, serving them soup and tea when they are sick. The elderly, in turn, are delighted to help with homework, plait the girls' hair into neat braids for school or help to wrangle the boys onto the school bus every morning. Laundry flapping on rooftop clotheslines and children scurrying across the courtyards wielding giant silver kettles of spicy chia tea give the place a feeling of home.

'It's a really special bond,' says Thinlay Ngodup who runs the home. 'It's beautiful to watch sometimes.' Which is just as well, as the endlessly patient 'Mr Thinlay', as the team calls him, oversees everything from homework, to dentist appointments and spiritual care. The resident jack-of-all-trades, he seems to be in perpetual motion. Past the dormitory rooms where the elderly live, two single beds to a room with a small Buddhist shrine in between, a group of elderly women quickly douse out smoke puffing out of a small cooker set up on the veranda.

Thinlay gently rebukes them. 'They like to cook their own dumplings or make tea, even though they're supposed to wait for the proper meals in the kitchen,' he says. 'They can be quite naughty sometimes.' An elderly lady, about 4-foot high, hobbles over on her walking stick, gives a huge toothless grin, grasps Thinlay's hands tightly and leans in for a hug. 'See you tomorrow!' she says brightly, trying out one of the few phrases of English she knows.

In the boys' dormitory, Thinlay stops to check the temperature of a sick seven-year-old curled up with the flu under a blanket on the bottom of a bunk bed. Then it's down a short flight of stairs to where the eye patients are temporarily housed, sitting around chatting, eating and resting on thin mattresses. He tousles the hair of an elderly man resting with patches on both his eyes after a cataract operation this morning. 'Today, he can hardly see, but tomorrow he'll be a free man,' he says. 'They don't have to suffer anymore the way they used to. The operation is so fast, and the results are so good. Dr Ruit operated on my father, who passed away last year at the age of 102. Right up until the end, Dad used to sit on the veranda right here, and his eyesight was so good that he could thread the needle for his own sewing.'

In the main courtyard, surrounded by bright pink bougainvillaea and white trumpet flowers, he points to small buildings where, once some of the orphans have graduated from school, they hope to run an optometrist, a pharmacy, a clothes alteration shop and a cafe. 'It's just one acre, but it's supporting so much life,' he says.

Every morning, when the mist rolls away, the 90 elderly folk and children enjoy front-row views of the snow peaks. In the monsoon season, watching the clouds roll overhead is like a spectator sport.

Certainly, it's a life-transforming place for the blind. Vibek Chettri, a local lawyer who helps organise many of the outreach camps, says the area is so impoverished that they realised the best way to attract a lot of patients to the eye camps was to advertise free meals. 'They would come just to have one solid meal for a few days, and while they were here we'd check their eyes and then offer free surgery if they needed it,' he says. 'Many of them became so much happier simply because they finally had enough to eat.'

Many of the elderly living in remote villages are both poor and illiterate, making it too expensive for them to travel to the hospital. Many are resigned to cataract blindness as an inevitable part of ageing. 'They're just so used to old people going blind, they accept it as their fate or a sad part of life,' Chettri says. 'They look almost spellbound when they place their trust in Dr Ruit and discover that they can actually see the world again.'

It's October 2016, and more than 170 people seeking help from Ruit are making their way up the steep road to the Jamgon Kongtrul Eye Centre at the Memorial Home. They've shuffled here clutching onto the back of a friend's shirt or dress hem. They have caught buses, sat on the back of motor-bikes, or been carried on the backs of their relatives to reach this one-acre sanctuary.

Despite the fact that most of them are in dire need, with bandages over their eyes, the atmosphere is festive. Many of the women wear silk saris and jewellery, and the men wear *topis*, a type of cotton hat. They sit in the sun, chatting among themselves and sipping chia tea. Perhaps it is the patients' unadulterated faith in the doctor, many of whom regard him as a living medicine Buddha, which creates such a joyous atmosphere.

The first day's surgery brings one particularly challenging patient, Chandra Maya, who is in a state of abject misery as she waits for her operation. Chandra has not only lost her sight, she is deaf and mute as well. Her face is as expressionless as a stone. She is about as utterly withdrawn from life as someone can be. As the pre-operation nurse examined her, it was hard to tell if she was asleep or awake.

Trapped in a silent dark world, her only guide is her husband Suresh. His weathered face, already etched with hardship from a life as a subsistence farmer, is creased with worry. Since Chandra went blind more than a year ago, he has had to take over his wife's role looking after their four grandchildren, who were left in the couple's care after their daughter died. He's had to stop farming to run the household. Their income has shrunk. In villages like Chandra's in northern India, where women are the lynchpin of the household, you can only imagine how devastating the blow of blindness is, and how demeaning it is for her not to be able to carry out her usual household tasks.

The surgical team's immediate problem, however, is how to prepare Chandra for surgery. Suresh gently strokes his wife's hand, but no-one is able to tell her what's about to happen.

'Operating on ladies like this is very difficult,' Ruit says. 'That's when I need a truly caring team around me. How do you communicate to someone like that that we are going to operate on her eyes? Often it is through touch. It is really only because my team is so special that we can do things like this.'

At first, the nurses and local monks who have put away their prayer beads to help with the patients have trouble getting Chandra to lie still enough to give her the anaesthetic block behind her eyes. She struggles and squirms, especially when they place a green hospital drape over her face. Then, a little miracle occurs; slowly, quietly, the nurses calm her down by gently stroking her face and hands. One nurse lifts up the green surgical drapes covering her head, and whispers in her ear, hoping the vibrations reassure her. It works. Without words, without sight, Chandra has somehow understood that she is being cared for, and she calms down, lying still on the operating table so that Ruit can get to work.

Ten minutes later, the operation is finished, and her husband leads her out of the operating theatre.

The fact that a special visitor is arriving is also creating a buzz of anticipation.

Princess Beatrice, the 28-year-old eldest daughter of Prince Andrew and Sarah, Duchess of York, has decided to come calling and see Ruit's work up close. Ruit quickly nodded in agreement when one of his supporters, the British film producer and businessman Simon Franks, mentioned he'd like to bring along the British princess, one of his and his wife's friends, to watch Ruit's life-transforming surgery.

Princess Beatrice, seventh in line to the British throne, is not the first high-profile person to show interest in Ruit's work. 'For some reason, people seem to believe in my work,' Ruit says. 'Somehow I feel there is something in me that people believe. I'm not sure what it is. You'd have to ask them yourself. They seem to believe I am stable and sincere, and I have some potential. They can see that I'm going to carry out future projects. I've found that by simply staying with my work, staying transparent, and keeping everyone up to date, people tend to stick with me. They believe in the work. They can see how focused I am, and that my direction is very clear, and that even though there are going to be hurdles, I'm going to overcome them.'

Princess Beatrice has lent her profile to several worthy causes, but she'd certainly never made such a bone-jarring road trip for charity before. Every security measure has been followed, and her bodyguard, Dominic Ryan, who was the former bodyguard of Prince Charles, stays within a metre of her side the entire trip. But no bodyguard can protect a princess from the nausea-inducing hairpin bends of the seventeen-hour mountain road from Kathmandu to Kalimpong.

Over dinner that night, the princess is bright-eyed and good-humoured, and talks of how much she enjoys her work in New York as a management consultant, well away from the prying eyes of the British media.

The princess's visit is certainly not incognito in Kalimpong. The whole town is buzzing with anticipation. Every Indian and Nepali newspaper ran front pages of her visit to the Tilganga Institute of Ophthalmology in Kathmandu a few days earlier.

Among the Nepalese chatter, you can frequently hear the word 'princess'. Balconies have been given a lick of fresh paint, and the highway is checked by police as the princess's entourage grinds its way up the last several hundred kilometres of serpentine road. On a tour of Tilganga, she had admired the 'Robin Hood effect' it provides, whereby free treatment and surgery is offered to tens of thousands of people a year, subsidised by the patients with good incomes who can afford it.

Shortly before her arrival, several red-robed monks from Jamgon Kongtrul's nearby monastery formed a welcoming party, bringing giant Tibetan drums, long trumpets, and incense into the courtyard. The orphans, thrilled to have the morning off school, and to meet a real live princess, scampered about in sequinned Indian saris. Ruit watched this scene of mayhem with amusement from the balcony above, and said jokingly, 'Why don't they organise something like that for me when I turn up, hey? Do I have to be a prince to receive such a welcome?'

When the princess's white LandCruiser finally pulled up to a halt in the courtyard, she emerged from the small cramped seat in the back cabin. As she explained rather charmingly later: 'I was smallest of the group, so it was best for me to take the smallest space.' The orphans went wild with excitement, festooning her with so many traditional scarves of welcome that she almost disappeared under white silk.

She's a seasoned speechmaker and before she's even had time to sit down to lunch, she gives a press conference for the coterie of reporters and cameramen gathered on the lawn. 'I'm really interested in promoting community eye centres like this one. To travel with Dr Ruit into the field like this is a huge opportunity and honour. I am so lucky to have had the opportunity to come and see the great work that is being done on the ground. It's a great chance to see the difference that can really be made. There was a young boy in Kathmandu who had a double cornea operation, and seeing how sight has transformed his life is a true inspiration.'

Ruit didn't hear a word. He was already back inside the operating theatre, having resumed the day's caseload of more than 70 patients. Before he went into the surgery, he carefully picked up his plastic sandals and took them with him, keeping them close by. At a previous camp, he'd left them in the changing room outside with everyone else's shoes, and they'd gone missing. 'Nanda will be very cross with me if I lose another pair,' he says sheepishly.

At dinner that night, he's completely at ease with the princess but looks down bashfully when she stands at the head of the table and praises his work.

'I thought it was fantastic for someone like that to come all that way to see our work and see how she could help,' Ruit says later. 'I thought it showed great commitment from her side. For somebody who was born in the best-dressed circles to come to meet people who are blind and almost bedridden was wonderful. She has come from one extreme of the world to the other.'

The next day, the patches are taken off Chandra with about 70 other patients. The 'Patches Off' ceremony, as it's known (even in Nepalese), is usually a spine-tingling half hour held every morning at the camps, and this one is particularly moving. It's a cool morning, and the ramparts of the Himalayas are swathed in mist.

The air is filled with excitement and anticipation as the patients sit quietly together on plastic chairs in the courtyard, still bandaged and patched. There is an extra frisson in the air as Princess Beatrice arrives to witness yesterday's work. Ruit is particularly keen to see the results of his handiwork on Chandra. After he unwinds her bandages, she looks confused, then almost wonderstruck as her line of vision slowly expands and she realises she can see the woman sitting next to her, and then, a metre away, standing right in front of her, her devoted husband Suresh. She starts nodding and smiling, seemingly unable to believe her good luck. Princess Beatrice leans in, obviously impressed by this stirring scene.

'It was at that moment you suddenly understand the dramatic impact of Dr Ruit's work. It was incredibly moving,' she says later. 'Having the chance to see first-hand Dr Ruit restoring a person's sight was truly remarkable.'

But it is Ruit's smile that is the widest. Thinlay puts it this way: 'This is it. This is what Dr Ruit loves. He loves to be with his patients. You can see it gives him such great satisfaction and that's what he really thrives on. It means much more to him than fame or money. That smile from the patient, that's what he truly lives for. It just brings him so much happiness.'

Thinlay explains that after meeting Ruit and witnessing the compassion the eye doctor showed the destitute, the 3rd Jamgon Kongtrul quickly wanted to become one of Ruit's major patrons, funding the new operating theatre of Tilganga, as well as a succession of remote eye camps such as this one. Ruit in return regarded him as a source of deep inspiration and was absolutely devastated by his untimely death in 1992. The 3rd Jamgon Kongtrul was only 37 years old and had spent his life dedicated to the welfare of others.

Ruit says, 'I remember when I first met Rinpoche, at his monastery in Kathmandu. We were sharing a cup of tea and talking, and I started getting a very strong personal aura from him. It was very interesting, as if I was being pulled toward him, and everything else in my life sort of faded away and every word he said seemed to be extremely important. He had a simplicity about the way he talked that you could never forget. He would say, "I'm building a monastery here," and, somehow, it's hard to explain, but it seemed very important information. Every word seemed important. He believed very strongly in social welfare, that building orphanages and schools and homes for old people was just as important as a monastery full of a thousand monks saying prayers and meditating.'

Jamgon Kongtrul's ashes were placed in a stupa or white-domed shrine at the Pullahari monastery, which he built, north of Kathmandu. Since his death, his work, through his foundation, the Jamgon Kongtrul Foundation, remains one of Ruit's greatest supporters. 'I still feel very strongly connected to him,' Ruit says. 'We have big photographs of him in our rooms at the hospital. What I remember the most was that whenever we talked about me increasing my work, reaching more patients, I saw a spark of light in his eyes. It was a fantastic spark in his eyes that [meant] it was something I really needed to follow.'

The seemingly miraculous quality of Ruit's work also captured the imaginations of Mei and Chiu Chi Wen, who met the doctor through Gabi Hollows. The couple are human dynamos, running their charity, Wen Giving, as well as property development companies in both Kuala Lumpur and Perth, Australia. As well as funding many of Ruit's eye camps, they donated a four-wheel drive to the hospital and provided more than fourteen ophthalmology scholarships at Tilganga. Now they're digging even deeper. They have joined Ruit in Kalimpong because they have promised to upgrade the Jamgon Kongtrul Eye Centre. They have also put $1.5 million on the table to fund Ruit's first community eye hospital in Bhutan, which is expected to open in 2018.

Ruit proved to be the perfect conduit for the couple's desire to help the impoverished country. Mei, a stylish, whip-smart woman with a wicked sense of humour, says: 'I used to visit Kathmandu when it was just a shack at the airport with a corrugated iron roof. I knew I wanted to do something to help early on when I watched a girl walking barefoot along the road. She was such a scrawny, skinny little thing, and her basket was bigger than her, and I couldn't stop thinking about what life was going to be like for her. It just tugged at my heart. As soon as we met Dr Ruit, we knew this was the way we could help girls like her.

'We were absolutely amazed by what he was doing. He's just consumed by his work restoring sight and he does it again and again. He just doesn't give up. It's a unique combination of heart and technical skills. We felt that with our backgrounds, from Malaysia and Singapore, we had an understanding of the Nepali culture and society he's come from and could really appreciate what he's done with his life. He has such a bold vision and he's translated that into a reality. It's not an easy thing to do, so we wanted to help him take more steps forward.'

Chiu Chi says, 'What's powerful about Ruit's work is the simplicity of purpose. You may not be able to change the world, but Ruit is showing us that fixing one big problem really is possible—you can let the blind see. His work has got that "wow" factor. You can see, hear, taste and smell the effect of his work. It's immediate gratification; the patients come in blind and when they come out, they can see. Once we came to the camps and saw what he was doing, it seemed impossible not to help. It's deeply moving.'

26

A LAND CALLED PARADISE

One of the rewards of Ruit's work is the special connection he has forged with Her Majesty the Queen Grandmother of Bhutan, Kesang Choden. Visiting her in the exotic Himalayan kingdom wedged between China and India always restores and rejuvenates his spirits.

His shoulders slump with relief as his team's two Toyota LandCruisers, each marked with a green 'H' for hospital, lumber across the border into the world's last Shangri-La in 2016. The vehicles and roof racks are crammed with thousands of dollars worth of surgical equipment and, despite the team having all their visas and papers, the border guards insist on checking everything. Ruit's team can't afford to have anything confiscated or rejected. And they certainly don't want any delays.

'It's always a tense half hour or so, even though we do everything properly,' Ruit says, using the break during the long day's drive across the mountains of northern India to phone Nanda in Kathmandu.

As his travelling surgery passes through the ornate gates into the Dragon Kingdom, it is as if a curtain of peace descends. Behind is the dusty mayhem of a typical Indian border town, the road gridlocked by men pulling rickshaws, gaudily decorated trucks, incessantly beeping buses, stray dogs barking, policemen wielding truncheons and vendors selling chunks of watermelon from trays on the back of pushbikes.

Within a few minutes inside the border of Bhutan, the air is suddenly pure and fresh, and the temperature cools as the convoy wends its way along the serpentine road toward the capital of Thimphu. Ahead is a six-hour drive through dense forests of pines, fir, juniper and spruce trees; more than 60 per cent of the kingdom has been preserved as a national park, making it the only country in the world which is not merely carbon neutral, but carbon negative.

At times, the mountain passes are so narrow, and the cliffs dropping into the valley below so vertiginous, that the Bhutanese official who had alighted at the border is forced to lean out the window to check how close the tyres are to the edge. He knocks loudly on the side of the vehicle to let the driver know if he can proceed or not. In some cases, it looks like there is only one, or maybe two centimetres to spare.

Despite this unnerving procedure, and the hair-raising bends which leave one of the nurses doubled over on the side of the road with motion sickness, the scenery is breathtaking. Amid the forest are waterfalls, rushing rivers and streams, dramatic rock formations, and small timber homes with pitched roofs. It looks like an Asiatic version of Switzerland; the houses could be alpine chalets except they have highly ornate windows carved out of timber, and the roofs are decorated with prayer flags. Nestled inside the ledges of rocks on the sides of the road are thousands of *kutzups*, tiny Buddha-like statues fashioned by monks out of the ashes of the recently departed.

There is a saying in Bhutan to 'take the best from the West and leave the rest', and each of the last five kings of the Wangchuck dynasty has done exactly that, implementing the best of modern life as they cautiously opened up their kingdom to the world. It's not perfect, but it's hard to find fault. In 1907, the first king, Ugyen Wangchuck, united the warring tribes, encouraged trade, built roads and set up the first non-monastic schools. The second king built bridges and medical facilities. The third established an independent judiciary and had a telephone network installed. But it was the previous king, 'K4' as he is known, the son of Her Majesty the Queen Grandmother, who pushed Bhutan into the world's consciousness by famously declaring that 'gross national happiness' was a more accurate measure of his kingdom's progress than amassing material wealth through gross domestic product. He also brought in hydro-electricity, social media and high-end tourism, allowing a privileged few to explore the kingdom's temples, forts, monasteries and wildlife for US$250 a day.

There's an appealing timelessness about Thimphu. Many of the locals still walk rather than drive to their destinations. They seem completely at ease wearing the national costume as they go about their daily business. The women wear *kiras*, slim-fitting, ankle-length tunics, worn over silk blouses, set off with an ornamental clasp on the shoulder. The men look equally polished in *ghos*, knee-length striped gowns, with long socks and leather dress shoes. The *ghos* are ingeniously practical; the entire lining above the waistline is an enormous pocket in which men keep mobile phones, papers, glasses, wallets and even iPads.

Every morning, hundreds make their way before dawn to temples or *chortens*, large white bell-shaped monuments topped with golden spires. Many perform prostrations on wooden boards inside the temple grounds, complete with hand and knee pads to protect themselves from splinters and blisters. They do these as unselfconsciously as a group of people doing their morning exercises or attending boot camp, and it is unfailingly moving to watch such open-air devotion.

'You can see why I have great respect for Bhutan, and the royal family,' Ruit says. 'It's in a precarious situation, bounded on three sides by India—and the other [side] by China—but they have such a strong sense of unity because of the royal family, and they seem to keep getting it right. There is a great reverence for the monarchy by the people because they, in turn, are truly devoted to the people. It's hard to find too much that is negative. You hardly see any beggars, and education and health are more or less free.'

As the Australian writer Bunty Avieson puts it her book, *The Dragon's Voice: How modern media found Bhutan*, 'The way the Bhutanese speak about their kings, they sound like a cross between living Gods and benevolent uncles who are very much part of their lives.'

By Ruit's side on this trip is his 26-year-old daughter Serabla, whom he affectionately calls 'The Boss'. After returning home from Kuala Lumpur with her business degree, she had been quietly assuming the role of her father's unofficial manager. She runs his new private clinic, which he moved to after his previous clinic of more than 20 years was destroyed by the earthquake. She also runs the Kathmandu office of Wen Giving, the charity set up by Mei and Chiu Chi Wen, who, in turn, affectionately call Ruit 'Dad'.

For Serabla, sitting in on the meetings to discuss the building of the new hospital in Bhutan—some of which are robust—is part of an unofficial apprenticeship.

Ruit treasures his relationships with his three children. Sagar graduated from medicine and was accepted to do his postgraduate ophthalmic degree at Tilganga (the Tilganga Institute has classrooms, a lecture hall and offices for 25 surgical fellows to use during their training.) Satenla, a third-year medical student at Manipal University in Pokhara, is following in the footsteps of her elder brother. But he has drawn particularly close to Serabla since she returned home and says she is a great comfort to him when he's on the road. 'More and more, I'd like family around me,' he says. 'There's always an outlet when things get stressful, isn't there?' he says, looking at her. 'I get comforted when my daughter is here. She cools me down. All I have to do is look at her face and I get total relief.'

Serabla is travelling with her father and helping out at the camps along with his team members, who have been with him for twenty years. Occasionally it rankles her to be known as 'Dr Ruit's daughter', but most days, she says, it is much more of a blessing than a burden.

So, did the three of them feel any pressure to be successful because of their famous father? 'My brother probably feels a bit of pressure, mainly because he's the eldest,' she admits. 'But Mum and Dad never made us study anything we didn't like. They always felt we should make careers out of what we enjoyed the most. Dad actually tried to talk Sagar and Satenla out of doing medicine, but they both really wanted to do it. They're strong-willed, like Dad.'

Between Ruit's feet on the floor is a small black backpack in which he keeps his passport, wallet, glasses, two mobile phones, sunglasses, cloth cap and fleece jacket. In the small zipped pocket at the front is a compact silk pouch containing lucky charms from two of his gurus. He pulls out the contents for closer inspection. First, he unfurls a wad of prayers printed on long rectangular strips of paper, given to him by the Tibetan Buddhist teacher Chatral Sange Dorje Rinpoche, who died in 2015 at the age of 104. 'I carry this with me everywhere,' he says, before quickly returning it inside the pouch.

Also tucked carefully inside is the preserved cataract of the Hindu saint, Yogi Naraharinath, who died in 2010 at the age of 92. 'I operated on him, and we used to have wonderful talks. The sense of him is still there in that little piece of him. He used to tell me that real leadership is like being inside a glass box, meaning that I needed to be transparent. If you want to be a leader then you have to be seen by everybody. Around the clock, even in your dreams. You need to set a good example both in your personal and professional career. He used to say he didn't know if there was a real God, but there are a lot of good people. The important thing about a belief in God is that you become accountable to somebody. He also said to steer away from too much material wealth because you can't take anything with you when it's time to go. What you take is your character and your good deeds; what you have done to help others. Both teachers really understood the value of my work. They both used to say restoring sight is just as important as saying prayers and mantras. They used to say the measure of a truly successful life is how many people you have helped, especially marginalised ones.'

Through Her Majesty the Queen Grandmother's patronage, Ruit and Tabin have been able to make an impressive dent in the backlog of the blind in the kingdom.

Ruit's voice drops into a reverential whisper as he describes his first meeting with Her Majesty in 1990.

'I was invited to lunch at her palace and was struck by how kind she was. She was so thoughtful, asking many questions about my work, and was concerned that I'd had enough to eat and drink. Over a period of time, I have developed a very interesting chemistry with Her Majesty. Somewhere I have a feeling that I could talk to her the way I talked to my own mother. Every time I come to Bhutan, I get totally inspired and energised. It's difficult to explain but I get this very strong feeling of great strength whenever I visit her. Every time I return, she says, "Doctor, I pray for you and your work every day." And who says that sort of thing to you, apart from your own mother, hey?'

Ruit was forthright asking for her support for his ambitious project. 'I said she would have to be our guiding force throughout and she said, "Of course doctor, of course!" You can see why I have a great respect for Her Majesty and a great love of Bhutan, can't you?'

The Queen Grandmother's home, Dechencholing Palace, is a handsome sandstone residence in the lush foothills seven kilometres north of Thimphu. Around it is a rambling garden, which in the drizzling rain seems reminiscent of the

English countryside. The Buddhist lama Dzongsar Khyentse Rinpoche, who visited often, adored the 'wild element' to the garden—recalling that on one of his visits he saw two bear cubs running around.

After being ushered up the wide stone steps by her aide-de-camp, a former paratrooper in full military uniform, guests are ushered through the grand entrance hall into the ground floor sitting room. With its plush silk sofas, expansive views of the forest, and side tables stacked with history and poetry books, it's a room that exudes great charm and in which visitors could happily stay for hours. The pale yellow walls are covered with photographs or paintings, each one with a story or special meaning.

One of these is a photograph of her main teacher, Kyabje Dilgo Khyentse Rinpoche, the spiritual giant who was the Dalai Lama's main teacher. He lived in Bhutan for more than 30 years, after fleeing Tibet. She was his lifelong devoted student and patron; Rinpoche lived in Dechencholing Palace for some time, and his presence is still strong. She looks up to the photograph several times when talking.

'It was through Dilgo Khyentse Rinpoche's grandson, Rajam Rinpoche, who has a monastery in Kathmandu, that we heard about Dr Ruit,' she says, making sure that afternoon tea is served meticulously with a fine bone china teapot, cups and saucers, sugar bowl and milk jug. Her voice is mesmerising—so soft, almost a whisper, so that you need to bend your head close to hear. At 86 she is still beautiful, her emerald silk gown setting off large black eyes that shine with intelligence and warmth.

'Everything that's been transformed in eye care in Bhutan

we owe to Dr Ruit's kindness and help,' she says. 'He is so full of love and compassion, and he has brought great blessings and joy to our country. He's my hero. We loved him very much as soon as we met him. Thanks to him, many, many people are able to see our beautiful country again, enjoy their lives again. We feel so proud that he is from the Himalayas and he has helped so many people by giving the gift of sight in places like Tibet, Bhutan and India. He works where people need him so badly. My daughter goes to his camps. He has helped train lots of our doctors, and he sends equipment, everything we need. We feel very fortunate to have met him.'

Her patronage—as well as the financial heft of the Himalayan Cataract Project—resulted in a dramatic transformation in eye health in the kingdom. When Ruit started working in Bhutan in the 1990s, there was only one ophthalmologist, Dr Kunzang Getshen. Today, more than nine eye doctors have been trained at Tilganga and more than 3000 Bhutanese patients can now see again.

As usual, Ruit is setting a cracking pace. On this trip, plans are being shored up to build Bhutan's first eye hospital, which will open in 2018, with 45 staff, and see more than 200 patients a day. It will be a replica of the district hospital Tilganga has already set up in Hetauda, in south-west Nepal, with an inbuilt cost recovery system whereby the operations will be free for those who can't afford it, paid for by those who can.

It will be the first of its kind in Bhutan—and the first of what Ruit hopes will be at least 30 similar district hospitals throughout the world; Nepal, India, China, Indonesia, Myanmar, Bhutan, and many parts of Africa. As HCP's

Job Heintz puts it, the community hospitals will 'replicate Nepalese ingenuity around the world'.

'It's very, very exciting,' says Ruit. 'It will set an example for other medical specialities to catch up to. The whole idea is to translate decades of our experience into a physical structure and to take it as a model that we will take to the developing world.'

In a quiet alcove of the lounge of the Hotel Druk in Thimphu, Harvard-trained architect Sanjay Bahadur Thapa and local Bhutanese architect Pem Gyaltsen have their heads bent low over a coffee table, poring over the sketches. In keeping with the rest of the town, the exterior of the three-storey structure will be built in the traditional style. The upper storey will be timber, with decorative window frames; there will even be an attic in which patients' families who have travelled from afar can store food, clothes and bedding. Inside, the screening rooms and operating theatres and recovery wards will gleam with modern hospital fixtures and cutting-edge technology.

For the unassuming Sanjay, whose portfolio includes five-star resorts and Indian universities, the Bhutan hospital, and the others to follow, are a 'lifelong' project, carried out for no payment, simply because he was inspired by Ruit's example.

'I've wanted to do my bit for a long time, and finally I found a way to do it. Dr Ruit has the ability to bring out the goodness in each of us. He provides the platform where all of us have been able to meet, interact, work together and feel good. It's an opportunity to give back. He seems to energise people from all over the world in a common cause. It's a true privilege to be associated with him and his work. He empowers people, he drives them, brings out the good in them. He'll give you his input but he doesn't interfere. And he has this uncanny knack of choosing exactly the right person for the right job to help him achieve his vision. I guess that's why I'm here.'

During this week of often tense discussions, Ruit calmly does 70 operations a day at the Thimphu National Referral Hospital, which looks more like a medieval fort than a medical facility. Ruit often works in picturesque places, and this one is breathtaking. On the mountain behind it, as if benevolently observing his every move, stands a 51-metre-high bronze Buddha, one of the largest of its kind in the world. All around in the emerald green slopes of the Thimphu Valley, thickets of long white prayer flags—'messages on the wind'—flutter jauntily, as if every day in the valley is a cause of celebration.

Inside the hospital, Ruit's team gown up in their dark green hospital scrubs and share a meal together of local red rice, curries, chicken dumplings, *ema datshi*, the local curry made with signature chilli and cheese, a local flat bread, and glasses of milk or tea.

Patient 31 this morning is a tall elderly woman with broad Tibetan features. Ruit falls unusually quiet as he props open her eye with a fine wire speculum and inspects the damage. A massive cataract has calcified into a rock-hard white mass in her right eye, obliterating her vision. Usually, Ruit will chat to his team, sometimes teasing them in a sing-song banter, as Bollywood classics play from speakers from his iPod.

But, in this patient's case, he goes into an almost trance-like state, utterly absorbed in the task of removing the disc, almost the size of a small coin. For twenty minutes, he remains as silent and still as a mountain, his hands making tiny delicate movements until he frees the cataract, cajoling it out of the lens through the tiny incision, before dropping it into a silver tray, to the palpable relief of everyone in the room.

'I get maybe two or three cases per hundred that are as difficult as that,' he says.

What is he thinking when he's dealing with such a case? 'I give it my all . . . Everything else I find secondary. Everything just falls away and I feel that I am dealing with the very life of the patient. I feel I have been given an opportunity, if I do it well, for the patient's life to be saved. I shut down everything else around me and focus on the safe outcome on the patient.'

Ruit is halfway through his pre-operation examinations the next day when Princess Ashi Kesang Wangmo Wangchuck stops to talk about the next outreach camps. Like most of her family, she's strikingly beautiful, with flawless skin, delicate features and silken black hair.

'I'll never forget the patients who looked up and said, "I can see! I can see again!" It's always such a wonderful moment,' the princess says. 'There is still a lack of awareness amongst some of the villages that, if you get to a clinic, and a doctor, you can have your sight restored. They think that God made them blind, so we are raising awareness that if you can come to one of Dr Ruit's camps or come to the hospital here, we can help them see again. We started from nothing and the ophthalmology here at the hospital has become the most modern facility in the whole hospital thanks to Dr Ruit. We love him because he is not arrogant. He's world famous but he comes across as the same as everyone else.'

27

DRAGON OF THE SKY

It wasn't until 2009, after many years of prompting by his cousin Tenzing Ukyab, that Ruit finally bought a substantial family home: a four-bedroom, two-storey house about ten minutes' walk from his parent's temple, Swayambhunath. As Nanda tends the peach, orange, lime, lemon and avocado trees in her front garden, she looks like she finally has everything she's ever desired. As a boy, Ruit would probably never have imagined he would end up living in such a comfortable home in the heart of Kathmandu. And yet, just like the simple timber house he grew up in, high in the Himalayan village of Walung, his new home is permeated with the sound of tinkling bells and the chanting of prayers.

When the American journalist Lisa Ling covered a story on Ruit for *National Geographic,* she allowed the camera to pan around his cramped apartment, asking the viewers rhetorically, 'And where do you think one of the world's most famous eye doctors chooses to live?' Her motivation was to highlight his humility, but many of Ruit's friends found it confounding. Why *did* he live in such a modest place for so long?

As a successful businessman, Ukyab felt the injustice keenly. He explains it this way: 'The reason why Sanduk and Nanda stayed in what I called "a dump", close to the stinking Bagmati River, was a matter of priorities. Sanduk could have stayed in Kathmandu, concentrated on his private practice and been one of the most prosperous doctors in Nepal. If he had stayed in Australia or gone to the US, he would probably be a multi-millionaire. But instead he chose to stay and serve his own country, curing hundreds and thousands of people around the world from blindness. The reason he did not find a proper place for his family to live for so long was because he was always going about doing his free eye camps rather than making money from his private practice. And he didn't want to burden his relatives and others with his personal problems. After many years of staying in that small flat, I kept urging him to shift to a more comfortable place, if not for himself, then at least for his family. I told him that for once he had to stop thinking of others and think about himself. Finally, I managed to convince him and we went hunting for a proper house. We all felt he had sacrificed his own well-being for too long, and, quite frankly, I can't think of anyone more deserving.'

The catalyst to move to a better place finally came when Kasang was injured in a bus accident one morning on her daily trip to the Swayambhunath temple, leaving her with bruises and cuts to her face which Ruit had to stitch up himself. As Kathmandu's population began to swell, and the roads gridlocked with cars, trucks, buses, bikes and tuktuks,

Kasang and Sonam's daily pilgrimage had become increasingly dangerous.

When Ruit and his cousin found the house for sale through friends, they were both immediately seized by the idea of buying it. Ruit took a deep breath and a big home loan. His nervousness was quickly assuaged when he realised what a haven the place would quickly become for his whole family.

His sister Chhengjing, a single mother, moved in with her teenage daughter and, for many years, spent two hours every morning taking Sonam to the Swayambhunath temple. The masterstroke of the house was that Ruit's parents could simply get up from the living room, walk out the front gates, and within minutes, walk up toward the pine-studded hill and be spinning the smooth timber prayer wheels set deep into the temple's walls.

Ladenla also lived there for several months, before setting himself up in his own house in Kathmandu once his health was recovered.

With Serabla and Sagar living back at home after moving away to complete their degrees, and Satenla coming home during her university breaks, Ruit's house—and his life—is at full tide.

Kasang enjoyed some of the happiest years of her life there before she passed away in 2013 at the age of 85. She always took great pride in her eldest son's work. If she didn't know which country he'd been working in, or the latest award he'd received, her friends were quick to tell her. Her faith remained as undented as her husband's right up until the end; their days revolved around the temple, and followed the religious calendar, lighting butter lamps or donating to beggars

on auspicious days, and saying prayers for auspicious circumstances on the waxing or waning of the moon.

Sonam probably would have had no idea, as he trekked
across the Himalayas to take his seven-year-old son so far
from home to gain an education, that he would be living
under the same roof as his son 50 years later. If he had, he
could only have smiled. Sadly, about three years after they'd
settled into their room upstairs with a view of the temple's
golden spires, Kasang was diagnosed with stomach cancer.
A gastrectomy to remove part of her stomach was performed,
prolonging her life by two years.

'It was wonderful having Mum at home under our roof
during her last years, knowing she was so close to the temple,
with her family all around her,' Ruit recalls. 'We talked every
day, mainly about happy times. We held hands a lot. She
was usually cheerful, even though her life had almost run its
course. She would think of certain things she was worried
about. She'd say, "You'll have to look after this, my dear,
and you have to look after that." I was so lucky to have a
mother who was so devoted to me and my brother and sisters.
There's nothing quite as powerful as that unconditional love.
I always knew she believed in me and was always so supportive of my dreams. That gives you a lot of inner strength as a
person. I know Nanda does the same with our children. It's
the greatest thing you can give a child.'

Ruit was setting his usual furious pace at an Indonesia eye
camp when Nanda rang him to tell him that Kasang's health
had suddenly deteriorated and the doctors said they couldn't
operate again. Ruit flew back to Kathmandu on the first flight
available. The day he arrived, he was able to talk to Kasang

just before all her senses started to dissolve. Toward the end of that day, she was no longer able to talk, or see, but Ruit sensed she could still hear him.

'I held both her hands and told her that I loved her, and that our whole family loved her, and that she had done a wonderful job bringing us all up. I kept reassuring her that we would all be fine, and that she was free to leave us. The next day she passed away. I think she was waiting for me to come home and to reassure her that everything was going to be all right, that Nanda and I could take care of everything from now on, before she could finally let go.'

Just before she lost consciousness, Ruit and Sonam organised for two lamas, Namkha Rinpoche and Manage Rinpoche, to conduct a Buddhist ceremony to guide her soul in the afterlife. They kept her body at home for four days before cremating her at the convergence of two rivers in Kathmandu.

'I know Dad misses Mum a lot, they used to tease and joke with each other so much, so he was very quiet for quite a while after she passed away. He just kept to himself in his room, but, after a few months, he came good again. He's very devout, and one thing that made him very happy was that she died in the presence of a great teacher.'

At 90, Sonam has slowed down greatly, but his faith remains as deep as the Tamor River that charted the course of his treks to Tibet and India for decades. For the last two decades, after his daily temple visit, he would nap in his bedroom, then watch the Dalai Lama or World Wide Wrestling on his television. He's so deaf that he has to put his ear right up to the television set. Of late he has become forgetful, and is too weak to go to the temple. He stays at home and, on sunny days, sits in the garden. In the winter, Chhengjing or Nanda tuck blankets around him, and brew hot lemon and honey tea for him to sip. 'He's still very, very faithful,' Ruit says. 'His faith has kept him agile and healthy. He might forget to eat, but he never forgets to chant or to say his prayers. His devotion is part of him, it's always with him.'

~

After more than 30 years together, people often ask Ruit and Nanda what makes their marriage work. He puts it down to three things: a deep respect for each other, a great deal of trust, and an abiding love of their children.

'One of the things we were both very clear about was that we wanted to raise our children extremely well. Nanda gave up her job so she could be there for the children. She was very good at her job—she would have been the head of nursing if she had stayed. She's very meticulous, very smart, very good with people. But it was her choice to stay at home. In doing so, she has given the children—and me—great stability in our lives. She's a wonderful mother: she encouraged the three of them to succeed, but she didn't drive them, and all that hard work she's put into them has paid off.'

As is the case in many good marriages, Ruit and Nanda have slogged away through tough times, and gone on to outlive many of their problems. Both say the hardest time was when they returned to Kathmandu after eloping to Holland and Australia and were ostracised by both their families. The years when Ruit broke away from the establishment— as well as his battle with the bottle, and the insomnia and high blood pressure that accompanied the stresses of that time—also placed a considerable strain on the marriage. There was also the ongoing stress of travelling to dangerous, remote places with his field hospital, such as Mustang and North Korea—long before the instant communication of Skype and mobile phones.

What binds them together is uncompromised trust. 'The trust is just so incredibly important. I was never concerned during our times apart that Nanda would be attracted to someone else. And that goes for me, too. She knows that I'm faithful to her. Every year the trust between us has grown from strength to strength.'

Although her family is Hindu, Nanda has slowly adopted Buddhism.

'She has such a strong ethical character beyond any man-made religion anyway,' Ruit says. 'She's gentle and extremely well-mannered and always seems to know the best way to approach things with the family. Much of the wisdom of the two different faiths is exactly the same anyway. It's about being kind. She's a font of good advice; I can be headstrong and stubborn and really quite cranky, and she always calms me down, tells me the right thing to do. At the end of each day, I still love just being around her. The simplicity of her dress, the way she walks, the way she talks. The choice of colour of what she wears. I love her and admire her all the more, the older I've grown. I can't imagine life without her.'

It's not a perfect relationship by any means. As Nanda says: 'He gets angry when things don't go his way, and of course sometimes we might disagree about something.' So how do they resolve conflict? 'Usually I don't respond very much when that happens,' she says. 'I just don't say anything.

Then ten minutes [later] we are carrying on as if nothing has happened.' Resentments don't smoulder for too long.

They still love the simple pleasures of eating together, going to the movies, and they plan to go on more treks, preferably around Kanchenjunga.

Love after three decades together, says Ruit, is not the melodramatic passion it was in the early days when he was prepared to slash his wrist to win Nanda's heart. These days, there are many small acts of kindness. He likes to surprise Nanda with presents, such as a bag or a watch. 'She's quite fussy, so I know if she gives me a little laugh that she really loves it.' Nanda will cook one of his favourite meals, such as roast lamb or beef curry, if he grumbles he hasn't had enough meat.

Ruit says that after 30 years together, they are 'truly reaping the benefits' of their marriage. For many years, he rose early to play badminton several times a week until a knee injury forced him to stop. But now, every morning, he and Nanda rise at about 5.30 a.m. and walk together for an hour and a half. 'Walking together really helps nurture the relationship. As does talking. You have to talk about everything, from the big to the little things. Especially when you are apart.'

Most days, their feet take them to Swayambhunath. There, they light butter lamps at the feet of the three giant Buddha statues, who sit in serene and humble dignity next to the busy road.

They listen to the comforting whirr of the prayer wheels being spun by hundreds of local devotees. As they make their way up the 365 stone steps, one for each day of the year, they inhale the familiar aroma of incense and juniper sprigs being burnt.

Over the last decade, as Ruit's work has spread around the world, his medical teams have operated on patients with multitudinous beliefs; on Muslims in Indonesia, Hindus in Nepal, Buddhists in Bhutan, and Christians in Ethiopia. The ancient temple of Swayambhunath, which pulses with spiritual power, also welcomes all faiths. As well as both Hindu and Buddhist shrines, a small Christian chapel has been built on one side, and a mosque on the other. On clear days, when the pollution rolls away like a veil, you can see how beautiful Kathmandu Valley must have once been, it's rough and lovely maze of homes and offices punctuated by white and gold temples encircled by the greatest mountain range on earth.

They both love the early morning light when the temple is lit up with thousands of tiny butter lamps and the place thrums with the murmured invocations of *Om Mani Padme Hum*. This is what Ruit misses, apart from his family, whenever he's travelling, and it is the first place he seeks whenever he comes home. It is a place of profound consolation that never fails to restore him. 'I don't know how it works, but it always drains away anything that happened the previous day.'

Once at the top, Ruit and Nanda thread their way among the golden spires and the forest of prayer flags flapping crisply in the breeze. Sometimes they might talk about the children, but often they just walk together in companionable silence. Ruit is a man of seemingly indomitable energy who, despite all he has already achieved, still has much to give to the world. But just for a few minutes every morning, he lets go, and, with Nanda by his side, stops for a few moments to take in the view of the eagles soaring effortlessly over the valley. He is Sanduk, Dragon of the Sky, after all, and this is his realm.

EPILOGUE

Wiping out avoidable blindness is an audacious vision. Many people have said it could never be done. Slowly but surely, however, by sticking to the task with doggedness and dedication, Ruit and his international medical teams are tackling the world's backlog of people who are needlessly blind. It might not happen next year, or even in the next decade, but this great injustice—something that affects more than 30 million people around the world—will one day be a thing of the past.

Already in the last 30 years in Nepal, Tilganga has halved the number of people who are blind in Nepal. The rates have gone down from 0.8 to 0.4 per cent of the population. Although cataracts are not something that can ever be truly wiped out, as they are a natural part of ageing, the ones that Ruit and his teams see now are far less mature. Of course, he hasn't been able to do this alone. The results are the collective determination of powerful organisations supporting him including The Fred Hollows Foundation in Australia, Vision Himalaya in

Switzerland, and the Himalayan Cataract Project in the United States.

Despite the abundance of feel-good patient stories, it is often the economic logic of restoring sight that prompts business people to support Ruit. More and more, Tilganga is about sitting down with finance ministers as well as health ministers to show in hard-headed terms that investing in vision is a huge boost for the economy. A study by Pricewater-houseCoopers showed that every dollar invested in restoring sight in a developing nation generated more than four dollars in economic benefits. Restoring sight has the same economic value to a community as providing primary school education and building bridges.

The good news is not just found in Nepal. The world is on the threshold of seeing the end of avoidable blindness. The 2013 Global Burden of Disease Study showed that, between 1990 and 2010, the combined effects of the growing and ageing world population should have pushed the number of blind people northward of 51 million, rather than the 32.4 million the tally stands at today. Simply put, that means that an additional 18.5 million people can now see because of the work these medical teams are doing. Half of these are from cataract surgery.

If you would like to help Sanduk Ruit's work, go to: the Tilganga Institute of Ophthalmology at tilganga.org (in Nepal); the Himalayan Cataract Project at cureblindness.org (in the United States); or The Fred Hollows Foundation at hollows.org (in Australia).

POSTSCRIPT

Rex Shore died on 16 December 2017. For the previous three years he had lived within walking distance of Les and Una Douglas in Mission Beach, Queensland, having finally retired from 'The Cause'. He requested that his ashes be scattered in the ocean in front of their home. Les and Una hung Nepalese prayer flags down the path to the beach, lit incense sticks, and placed them in front of the small statue of Buddha which Rex always placed flowers on every time he visited. At Tilganga, Ruit and his staff commemorated his death by setting up a new award, The Rex Shore Community Award. 'I'm sure he would have loved to have been remembered this way. We all hold him in our hearts.'

ACKNOWLEDGEMENTS

I owe a great debt to author Sue Williams, who believed in this book as soon as I told her about it over a coffee in Kings Cross. Sue opened the door to publishing, and offered sterling advice whenever I faltered. She led by example, showing the true grit needed to write a book. I honour the late author David Oliver Relin, whose biography, *Second Suns*, laid the groundwork for my first interviews. My heartfelt thanks to Marianne Gizycki and Carolyn Parfitt for advice on the early draft. For their following people for their recollections, I am so grateful. In the United States: Lisa Ling, Richard Gere, Professor David Chang, Dr Dick Litwin, Professor Alan Robin, Professor Geoff Tabin, Job Heintz. In Nepal: Dr Reeta Gurung, Shankya Twyna, Nanda Ruit and Serabla Ruit. In Bhutan: Her Majesty the Queen Grandmother, Princess Ashi Kesang Wangmo Wangchuck, Dr Dechen Wangmo, Dr Kunzang Getshen, Matthieu Ricard, Mei and Chiu Chi Wen. In India: The office of His Holiness the Dalai Lama, Thinlay Ngodup, Princess Beatrice of York, Sanjay Bahadur

Thapa. In Australia: David Britton, Professor Hugh Taylor, Joel Edgerton, Les Douglas, Rex Shore, Mike Lynskey, Ray Martin, Gabi Hollows, David Moran, Indra Ban, Sarah Elliott, Catherine Marciniak, Pat Fiske. In New Zealand: Sir Ray Avery.

I owe special thanks to Michael Amendolia for 30 years of friendship and creative collaboration, for his world-class photographs and for introducing me to Dr Ruit. To ladies of letters Joyce Morgan and Elizabeth Fortescue for cheering me across the finishing line. And most importantly to my parents, Jillian and Terry, and my siblings Neil and Jane, Russell and Annabelle, and Anne and Dyanna, for a lifetime of love and support. Praise is due to Serabla Ruit for her superb translation and editing skills. Finally, to Sanduk Ruit, Dragon of the Sky, for taking me on the greatest ride of my life. Thank you for the honour of asking me to tell your story. May your work continue to strengthen and grow.

APPENDIX

The history of cataract surgery

Couching was the only technique available until the late 1700s when French ophthalmologist Jacques Daviel worked out a crude way to extract the calcified white discs known as cataracts. The results varied from good to disastrous. A 1-centimetre incision was made in the eye, and the lens removed, after which the wound was stitched up with large needles. The patients were forced to lie flat on their back for days with their heads wedged between two sandbags to stop them from moving. Later on, doctors used forceps or suction to capture the cataract, and the wound was closed with silk sutures, but these were minor improvements; infection rates were sky high.

After the lenses were removed, the patient was fitted with spectacles so thick that they were dubbed 'Coke-bottle glasses'. The patient could see, but only through a narrow tunnel, with very little peripheral vision. Everything was also magnified by about one-third, so objects such as a cup of tea or a stack of firewood would seem much closer than they really were. One patient described walking along steep mountain paths in them as 'like stepping into thin air'. If their glasses were lost, the patient was left completely blind. This technique was still the most common treatment used in Nepal until Ruit began performing modern intraocular surgery.

Internationally, the big breakthrough came in the 1950s, in St Thomas' Hospital, London, when British ophthalmologist Sir Harold Ridley came across a curious phenomenon. Operating on World World II fighter pilots, he noticed that despite their Perspex windshields shattering during enemy fire, the plastic fragments lodged in their eyes had not inflamed or damaged the tissue at all.

Dr Ridley went on to pioneer a revolutionary technique by creating artificial lenses which were implanted in the eye after the clouded old lenses were removed. By the late 1970s and early 80s, the lens became much smaller and more sophisticated, and the technique slowly gained widespread acceptance. It was regarded as the golden age of ophthalmology.

"One of the great joys of my life is having been part of the training of Sanduk Ruit and his training others."
– Fred Hollows

When Fred Hollows met Dr Sanduk Ruit in the 1980s he found a kindred spirit.

Both shared the same vision – to make eye care, particularly modern cataract surgery, accessible and affordable for the poorest people in the world. Together, they made it happen.

Their efforts to establish the Tilganga Institute of Ophthalmology and its revolutionary Fred Hollows Intraocular Lens Factory in Kathmandu dramatically reduced the cost of high quality cataract surgery for people in Nepal and other developing countries.

Now, The Fred Hollows Foundation can restore sight for as little as $25 in some countries.

4 out of 5 people who are blind don't need to be.
Just $25 can restore sight.
Donate at www.hollows.org or call 1800 352 352.